KNITTED
BIRDS

Dedication
Dedicated to Caroline Wilbor at
The Wool Bar, Worthing – your
generosity, support and kindness
gave this book its wings.

NICKY FIJALKOWSKA

KNITTED BIRDS

Over 30 fun feathered friends for you to knit

Search Press

First published in 2015

Search Press Limited
Wellwood, North Farm Road,
Tunbridge Wells, Kent TN2 3DR

Reprinted 2016, 2017 (twice), 2019

Text copyright © Nicky Fijalkowska 2015
Photographs by Paul Bricknell at Search Press Studios
Photographs and design copyright © Search Press Ltd 2015

ISBN 978-1-78221-109-9

Suppliers
If you have difficulty in obtaining any of the materials and equipment
mentioned in this book, then please visit the Search Press website
for details of suppliers: searchpress.com

You are invited to visit the author's blog: knitforvictory.co.uk

CONTENTS

INTRODUCTION 8

MATERIALS 10

TECHNIQUES 12

MALLARDS 18

  Adult male mallard 18
  Adult female mallard 20
  Mallard duckling 23

SONG THRUSH 24

BLUE TIT 28

CANADA GOOSE 32

BLACKBIRDS 36

  Adult blackbird 36
  Fledgling blackbird 38

MUTE SWANS 40

  Adult swan 40
  Cygnet 44

BARN OWLS 46

  Adult barn owl 46
  Barn owlet 48

AVOCET 50

LAPWING 54

PUFFIN 58

COLLARED DOVE 62

MAGPIE 66

OYSTERCATCHER 70

OSPREY 74

KINGFISHERS 80

HOOPOE 84

PHEASANT 88

SNOWY OWLS 94

WOODPECKER 98

ROBIN 102

SPARROW 106

SEAGULL 110

RAVEN 114

TUFTED DUCK 120

EGGS AND NESTS 124

  Eggs 124
  Nests 126

INTRODUCTION

This book began with an unusual request for a gigantic knitted seagull. Caroline, the owner of The Wool Bar, my lovely local yarn shop, wanted a life-sized knitted herring gull to sit in her window. How could I say no? The seagulls of Worthing were suitably impressed: on its first morning in the shop, I remember one of them peering through the window with a 'who are you?' look on his face. (There's a tiny knitted relative of the original gull on page 110 if you'd like one of your own).

After that, I started knitting some of the inhabitants of my local Wetlands Trust Centre at Arundel, UK. Ducks, geese and swans are wonderfully obliging models – beautiful, large, and slow-moving. You get plenty of time to observe their stunning details. If you are thinking of starting bird watching, water birds are a good place to start for this very reason!

I have included many of my favourite birds in this book, large and small, from friendly and familiar garden visitors like the robin, blackbird and blue tit, to more elusive birds like the hoopoe and the kingfisher. The largest birds in the book, like the osprey and the avocet, will make impressive knitted ornaments to keep next to your bird-watching binoculars. Smaller knitted birds with posable feet can cling to bird feeders, the edges of flowerpots, or perch among your houseplants. You could also make the little birds without wire legs and attach a loop of ribbon to their back to use as Christmas tree ornaments – robins would look particularly festive.

I am a keen bird watcher, but a terrible bird photographer. My mobile phone is full of blurry pictures of expanses of sand with a tiny white speck in the distance which may (or may not) be a little egret. There are also lots of photographs of trees where a blackbird was before I got too close and it flew off. These knitted birds are a gift to the lazy avian photographer. They will obligingly sit in a bush, or on the grass, for as long as you like, and let you get as close as you need to while you snap away. It is a lot of fun positioning the knitted birds in their natural habitat and playing around with your camera. I hope you give it a try! No enormous telephoto lens necessary.

All of the birds, eggs and nests in the book are worked flat, on two needles. One of the biggest challenges in writing the patterns for this book was finding a way of creating the aerodynamic curves of our feathered friends using only two needles. I hope you enjoy knitting a flock of your favourite birds as much as I enjoyed creating them!

A note on safety

As the birds in this book use wire, glass pebbles and beads in their construction, they are meant as ornaments rather than toys, and are not to be given to children. However, if you omit the glass pebbles and wire, sew the beaks on really firmly, and embroider eyes with thread rather than use beads, many of the knitted birds will make fantastic cat toys. Just don't tell me if you do this, I may cry.

MATERIALS

Here are some of the yarns, equipment and other materials that I used to create the birds in this book.

YARNS

For the most part, the birds are knitted with 8-ply (DK) yarn. The smaller birds are a perfect opportunity to use up any odds and ends of yarn that you have left over from other projects, as they use only a tiny amount of yarn to make.

I like to use a good quality yarn with a high percentage of natural fibre in it, like King Cole Merino Blend DK or Bessie May Smile yarn. However, the birds will work just as well if you use acrylic yarn. I have also used specialist yarns like Debbie Bliss Angel superfine mohair/silk blend for some projects. This yarn is used to give a downy texture to the fluffier birds. Substitute for another fine, fluffy yarn if necessary.

The lapwing pattern uses Patons Valiani shade 00069 which is dark green with a silver shimmer. If you can not find a substitute yarn, dark green 8-ply (DK) yarn will work as well.

To create the pheasant, I used Debbie Bliss Milano aran tweed yarn, (shade 49003 – brown, red, and orange speckle) for the rump and wing speckles and a golden brown tweed effect 8-ply (DK) yarn from Rowan Felted Tweed (Cinnamon: shade 175) for the back and wings, but you can substitute either of these for other tweedy, brown, speckly yarns.

I used Jamieson and Smith 2-ply (lace) yarn to knit the little blackbird eggs and also to add the black speckles to the magpie eggs. Substitute with any other 2-ply (lace) yarn. The magpie nest is lined with textured yarn – I used a skein of different textured lace-making yarn from Lacebobbins' Etsy store but you can use any quirky vintage yarns, ribbons or sparkly threads that you can find in your stash!

KNITTING NEEDLES

All of the birds are knitted flat, using a pair of 4mm (UK 8, US 6) needles. I like to use a small pair of round needles as they are shorter than standard knitting needles and easy to use on small projects. However, you can use any type of knitting needles of the right size to create your flock.

The tiny blackbird's eggs are made using 3mm (UK 11, US2/3) knitting needles. Again, you can use any type of needle. The bird's nests are worked on 5.5mm (UK 5, US 9) needles. I suggest you use an old pair of tough metal needles for these as you will be knitting with rough garden twine and you do not want to break your best wooden needles in the process!

OTHER MATERIALS

Crochet hooks 4mm (UK 8, US G/6), 3.5mm (UK 9, US E/00) and 5mm (UK 6, US H/8) crochet hooks are used to make short crochet chains for the barn owls and avocet.

Thread I have used natural pure cotton thread to sew on beaks, eyes and felt details. For wrapping some of the bird's legs, I have used stranded embroidery thread, or crochet cotton, as these threads are thicker than cotton on a reel, and easier to wrap with. The stranded embroidery thread also has a pretty sheen. If you do not want to use stranded embroidery thread or crochet cotton, you can use appropriately-coloured yarn.

Sewing/embroidery needles You will need a blunt darning needle to sew the birds' seams together and attach the wings. You will also need a small, sharp darning needle for wrapping yarn around the wire legs, and a small sewing needle for sewing up beak seams and attaching eyes.

Glass pebbles Some of the birds are weighted with glass pebbles to make the bird more stable. You can use marbles, or small, clean natural pebbles instead.

Beads These are used to create the bird's eyes. The size required is stated on each pattern. I like to use glass or wood beads but plastic ones will work just as well.

Wire Mainly used for the birds' feet and legs, you will need to use craft wire which is flexible enough to bend by hand but stiff enough to support the bird. Florists' wire or 18–20 gauge craft wire works well. If you use stiffer wire then you will need to use pliers to squeeze the toe loops closed.

Toy stuffing I have used polyester toy stuffing throughout the book, as it is light, and easy to use. Before stuffing your birds, fluff out your stuffing to get rid of any lumps.

Felt Felt is used for beaks, and on some birds, face and breast markings. I like to use a wool/viscose blend felt. This can be attached using strong white glue, or sewn on, as you prefer.

Chenille stems Also called pipe cleaners, these are wires covered with fabric. They tend to be sold in 15cm (6in) lengths and are used to help support wings and tails.

Scissors You will need a small, sharp pair of scissors for snipping yarn, and cutting out felt shapes. A small pair of wire cutters will also be useful for creating the birds' legs.

TECHNIQUES

The basic techniques on this and the facing page are used to make the duck shown to the right, but they apply more generally to almost all of the projects. Where modifications to the techniques are needed for a particular bird, this is noted in the text for the specific project.

MAKING FELT BEAKS AND BILLS

Most of the birds in this book have felt beaks made using this technique. The templates for each beak are included with the specific project patterns. Use a cotton thread to sew up the beak seams in the same shade as your felt.

1 Using the templates provided and a pair of scissors, cut out the required beak pieces from felt.

2 Place the lower beak on top of the upper beak, with one side aligned. Using a thread in the same colour as the felt, begin to sew up the seam on this side, starting from the base of the beak and working to the tip.

3 Align the free sides as shown to give the upper beak a curved shape. Holding it in place as you work, continue sewing round the beak down to the other end.

4 Secure and trim any excess thread. This completes the beak ready for stuffing (see opposite) and sewing on to the bird.

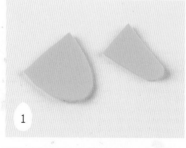

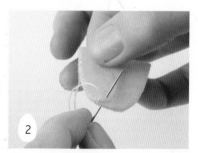

MAKING UP

The step-by-step instructions below show how to seam, stuff and weight your knitted bird. Some birds contain glass pebbles to make them more stable. It will tell you in the individual knitting pattern if you need to do this.

As you work, you can either use the loose ends from the knitting, or matching yarns to sew up the seam.

1 With your piece completed, fold it in half. Using a darning needle and a loose end of yarn, begin to sew up the bird, working from the crown of the head down towards the point of the tail.

2 As you work, use appropriately-coloured loose ends for the sections you are sewing up.

3 Continue working round the bird, down the back, round the tail and towards the belly opening. Leave a 5cm (2in) gap before the end.

4 Use a small amount of toy stuffing to stuff the head. Be careful not to overstuff your birds as this can distort the knitting so you lose the bird's shape. You can push in any loose ends at this point (or trim them off, if you prefer) to help fill the bird.

5 Stuff the rest of the bird gradually. Use small amounts of stuffing, and take your time to shape the body as you work.

6 If the bird requires weighting, add some glass pebbles once the bird is stuffed and shaped

7 Cover the glass pebbles with a little more stuffing.

8 Sew up the seam to close the hole and finish.

UNSUPPORTED TAILS

Many of the knitted birds have a tail that lies flat horizontally. Follow the instructions below and make sure that you flatten the tail to achieve the correct shape.

1 Sew the bird up along the belly line, stuffing as you go until you reach the base of the tail. Sew up the tail, adding no stuffing.

2 Use your fingers to flatten the tail as shown, so that the seam is in the centre.

3 Sew up the end of the tail to fix it in the horizontal shape, then sew in the loose ends to finish.

SUPPORTED TAIL

Some of the projects ask for a supported tail. This is worked in a similar way to an unsupported tail (see above) except that a chenille stem is inserted after the bird has been sewn up to the base of the tail.

1 Bend the end of a 15cm (6in) chenille stem over and wrap sticky tape around it to cover the sharp end.

2 Place the taped part on the tail, 0.5cm (¼in) away from the end. Use scissors to cut it 5cm (2in) past the end of the tail.

3 Push the trimmed end into the stuffing, then, working from the end of the tail towards the belly, sew up the bird to trap the chenille stem in place.

4 Once complete, sew up the end of the tail to fix it horizontally (see *Unsupported tails* above). The tail can now be posed.

POSABLE LEGS

These legs are flexible but strong enough for the finished piece to cling on to your finger, a branch or a piece of furniture. They are particularly suited to delicate garden birds or any small bird you want perching somewhere about your house.

1 Cut a length of craft wire (the gauge will be specified in the pattern). Using a sharp darning needle, thread the wire through the bird's body in the position where you want the legs to sit. Thread the wire through a good amount of stuffing – not just surface knitting – to give the legs more stability.

2 Remove the needle and position the wire so that it has an equal amount on each side of the bird.

3 Fold the wire into loops as shown to make four toes, each 2cm (¾in) long.

4 Twist the remainder of the wire on that side of the bird around the base of the toes to hold it in position, then repeat the process with the other half of the wire to create a second foot.

5 Thread a sharp darning needle with 60cm (23½in) of thread and secure it to the base of one of the feet with small stitches.

6 Wrap the yarn around one of the toes, wrapping it around both pieces of wire at the same time, until you reach the loop of wire at the end of the toe.

7 Use your darning needle to wrap the yarn around the single wire loop to stop the yarn slipping off the end of the toe.

8 Squash the wrapped wire loop flat, then work your way back down the toe, wrapping as you go. Repeat on the other three toes. Wrap the thread around the base of the toes to keep the foot together, then wrap the thread up the leg and secure it with a few small stitches in the knitting where the leg meets the bird's body.

9 Repeat on the other foot, then bend both into the right shape, with three toes facing forward, one facing back.

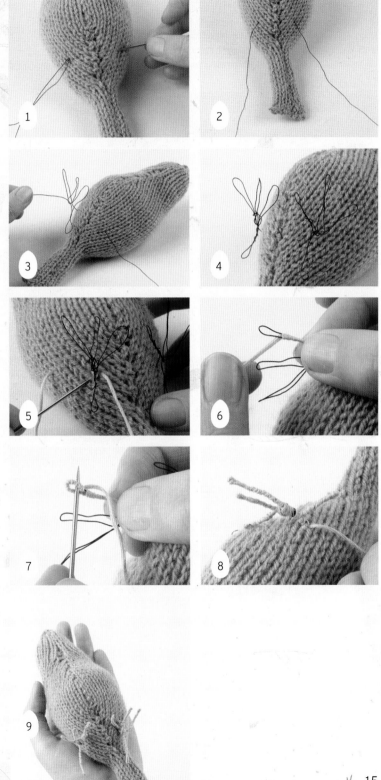

SUPPORTING LEGS

For larger birds that stand upright, particularly wading birds, you will need to use craft wire which is flexible enough to bend by hand but stiff enough to support the bird. 16–18 gauge florists' wire or craft wire works well.

1 Take a length of wire (the gauge and type will be specified in the pattern) and thread it into position through the bird's body, then fold the bird's feet exactly as for the posable legs (see page 15). Once you have formed the toes, twist a little of the excess wire around the base of the toes to hold it in place. Trim any excess.

2 Cut a 7.75–10cm (3-4in) length of wire and fold it into a hoop.

3 Insert the hoop into the belly on the side of the leg and secure with a little sticky tape. This wire acts as extra support to help the bird balance.

4 Do the same on the other leg, then place the bird on a flat surface and make small adjustments to the angle of the toes and legs until your bird stands up. Add some small weights to the feet to increase stability: adhesive putty, polymer clay, small screws or nuts will all work.

5 Wrap the legs using the same technique as for the posable legs (see page 15), but do not squash the toe loops when you have finished wrapping them. Keep wrapping the feet until you can no longer see the wire and weights.

6 To help give the legs extra support, oversew a few stitches where the leg meets the body, wrapping your thread around the leg and support wire, and securing it into the body. Use the same coloured yarn as the bird's belly. Keep oversewing until you can no longer see the support wire.

SWISS DARNING STITCH

Swiss darning is an embroidery stitch which looks like a knit stitch. Work the stitch to the same tension as your knitted piece. It is best to add Swiss darning once your bird is stuffed as the tension of the stitches will change when stuffed.

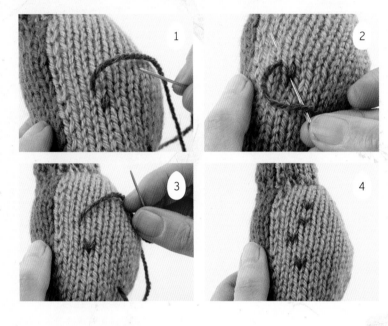

1 Thread a blunt darning needle with a length of yarn. Secure the yarn with a small running stitch, then bring the needle up where you want the first Swiss darning stitch to sit. Draw the yarn through and take it down a little above and to the left, to create a small stitch. Bring the yarn back up to the left of the top of the first stitch.

2 Take the needle back down at the base of the swiss darning stitch (where you first brought the needle up), then take it back out where you want the base of the next Swiss darning stitch.

3 Draw the needle through until the yarn sits in a neat 'V' shape to finish the first stitch.

4 Continue adding Swiss darning stitches in the same way. Once you have finished darning, secure your yarn with a running stitch and sew in the ends.

CROCHET CHAIN

Crochet chain is used to make neat borders and details for the barn owls and avocet.

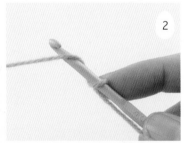

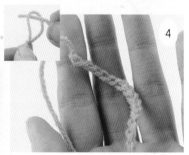

1 Take your yarn and create a slip knot, leaving about a 15cm (6in) tail of yarn. Insert your crochet hook into the slip knot's loop.

2 Hold the crochet hook in your right hand and your yarn in your left hand. Wrap the yarn around the crochet hook, from right to left, so there is a strand of yarn lying across the hook, just under the hook.

3 Pull the slip knot loop up and over the hook and the wrapped yarn. This is your first chain stitch.

4 Wrap the yarn again, pull your last stitch up and over the hook and the wrapped yarn. Keep repeating this step until the chain is the length required for your pattern. To end the chain, cut your yarn, leaving a 15cm (6in) tail. Pull gently on your crochet hook to make the final stitch loop a little bigger, then pull this tail though the loop (see inset). Your chain will now be secure. Use the ends to sew the chain into the bird,

MALLARDS

Here is a whole family of handsome mallard ducks to knit. It is easy to overlook the beauty of these birds – the male has an exotic glossy green head, and the female has a beautiful indigo flash on her wing – and of course, the tiny ducklings are adorable!

ADULT MALE MALLARD

NOTES
The colours in parentheses indicate the yarn you should use for the stitches that follow.

BODY AND HEAD (MAKE ONE)
Worked in st st. Using 4mm (UK 8, US 6) knitting needles and light grey yarn, cast on 14 sts.
Row 1: inc 1, K5, inc 2, K5, inc 1 [18 sts].
Row 2: purl.
Row 3: inc 1, K7, inc 2, K7, inc 1 [22 sts].
Row 4: purl.
From row 5 onwards, work with two balls of light grey yarn so you do not have to carry the yarn across the back of the dark brown section.
Row 5: (light grey) inc 1, K7, (dark brown) K2, inc 2, K2, (light grey) K7, inc 1 [26 sts].
Row 6: purl, keeping colour sequence.
Row 7: (light grey) inc 1, K8, (dark brown) K3, inc 2, K3, (light grey) K8, inc 1 [30 sts].
Row 8: purl, keeping colour sequence.
Row 9: (light grey) inc 1, K9, (dark brown) K4, inc 2, K4, (light grey) K9, inc 1 [34 sts].
Row 10: purl, keeping colour sequence.
Row 11: (light grey) inc 1, K10, (dark brown) K5, inc 2, K5, (light grey) K10, inc 1 [38 sts].
Row 12: purl, keeping colour sequence.
Row 13: (light grey) inc 1, K11, (dark brown) K6, inc 2, K6, (light grey) K11, inc 1 [42 sts].
Row 14: purl, keeping colour sequence.
Row 15: (light grey) inc 1, K12, (dark brown) K16, (light grey), K12, inc 1 [44 sts].

Materials
- Small amounts of 8-ply (DK) yarn in light grey (belly and wings), light brown (top of body), dark brown (chest), cream (neck ring), dark green (head), and black (tail)
- Two 3mm (⅛in) black beads
- Black cotton thread and sewing needle
- Small amount of yellow felt and matching cotton thread
- Two or three glass pebbles
- Toy stuffing

Needles
- 4mm (UK 8, US 6) knitting needles

Tension
- 6 sts and 7 rows per 2.5cm (1in)

Size
- 15cm (6in) long including beak, 10cm (4in) tall

Mallard bill templates

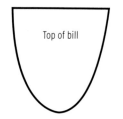
Top of bill

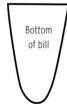
Bottom of bill

Row 16: purl, keeping colour sequence.
From row 17 onwards, work with two balls of black and two balls of light brown yarn.
Row 17: (black) inc 1, K3, (light brown) K10, (dark brown) K16, (light brown) K10, (black) K3, inc 1 [46 sts].
Row 18: purl, keeping colour sequence.
Row 19: (black) inc 1, K4, (light brown) K10, (dark brown) K16, (light brown) K10, (black) K4, inc 1 [48 sts].
Row 20: purl, keeping colour sequence.
Row 21: Cast off 16 sts knitwise keeping colour sequence, K to end, keeping colour sequence [32 sts].
Row 22: Cast off 16 sts purlwise keeping colour sequence, change to cream yarn and purl to end [16 sts].
Row 23: (cream) knit [16 sts].
Work in dark green from this point to the end of the head.

Rows 24–30: (dark green) beginning with a purl row, work st st.

Row 31: K1, *K1, K2tog*, rep from * to * to end [11 sts].

Row 32: purl.

Row 33: K1, then K2tog to end [6 sts].

Cut yarn, thread trailing end through remaining sts.

RIGHT WING (MAKE ONE)

Worked in st st. Using 4mm (UK 8, US 6) needles and light grey yarn, cast on 4 sts.

Row 1: inc 1, K2, inc 1 [6 sts].

Row 2: purl.

Row 3: inc 1, K4, inc 1 [8 sts].

Row 4: purl.

Row 5: inc 1, K6, inc 1 [10 sts].

Rows 6–8: beginning with a purl row, work st st.

Row 9: K to last 3 sts, K2tog, K1 [9 sts].

Row 10: purl.

Row 11: K to last 3 sts, K2tog, K1 [8 sts].

Row 12: purl.

Row 13: K to last 3 sts, K2tog, K1 [7 sts].

Row 14: purl.

Row 15: K to last 3 sts, K2tog, K1 [6 sts].

Row 16: purl.

Row 17: K to last 3 sts, K2tog, K1 [5 sts].

Row 18: purl.

Row 19: K2tog, K1, K2tog [3 sts].

Row 20: purl.

Cast off remaining sts.

LEFT WING (MAKE ONE)

Worked in st st. Using 4mm (UK 8, US 6) needles and light grey yarn, cast on 4 sts.

Rows 1–8: work as for right wing.

Row 9: K1, K2tog, K to end [9 sts].

Row 10: purl.

Row 11: K1, K2tog, K to end [8 sts].

Row 12: purl.

Row 13: K1, K2tog, K to end [7 sts].

Row 14: purl.

Row 15: K1, K2tog, K to end [6 sts].

Row 16: purl.

Row 17: K1, K2tog, K to end [5 sts].

Row 18: purl.

Row 19: K2tog, K1, K2tog [3 sts].

Row 20: purl.

Cast off remaining sts.

MAKING UP

Sew up the seam from the top of the head to the end of the tail. Stuff the head, and then sew up the seam from the end of the tail to the base of the bird, leaving a space for stuffing the body. Stuff the body, inserting two or three glass pebbles to weigh the base of the duck down and help give it stability. Tuck stuffing all around the pebbles so they do not poke through the knitted fabric surface. Sew up the belly seam.

   Sew the wings onto the body, with the straight edges of the wings positioned towards the top.

   Cut out two yellow felt beak shapes using the template and overstitch them together using yellow cotton thread, leaving the end that will attach to the head open. Stuff the beak with a little toy stuffing and sew it to the head. Sew the two black beads on to the head for eyes, using black thread and a sewing needle.

   Using black 8-ply (DK) yarn, make two 1cm (⅜in) tassels of thread at the end of the tail, for tail feathers.

ADULT FEMALE MALLARD

Materials

- ↯ 15g (½oz) light brown tweed effect 8-ply (DK) yarn
- ↯ Oddments of 8-ply (DK) yarn in cream and dark blue (wing flashes)
- ↯ Two 3mm (⅛in) black beads
- ↯ Black cotton thread and sewing needle
- ↯ Small amount of brown felt and matching cotton thread
- ↯ Two or three glass pebbles
- ↯ Toy stuffing
- ↯ Darning needle

Needles

- ↯ 4mm (UK 8, US 6) knitting needles

Tension

- ↯ 6 sts and 7 rows per 2.5cm (1in)

Size

- ↯ 15cm (6in) long including beak, 10cm (4in) tall

BODY AND HEAD (MAKE ONE)

Worked in st st. Using 4mm (UK 8, US 6) needles and light brown yarn, cast on 14 sts.

Row 1: inc 1, K5, inc 2, K5, inc 1 [18 sts].
Row 2: purl.
Row 3: inc 1, K7, inc 2, K7, inc 1 [22 sts].
Row 4: purl.
Row 5: inc 1, K9, inc 2, K9, inc 1 [26 sts].
Row 6: purl.
Row 7: inc 1, K11, inc 2, K11, inc 1 [30 sts].
Row 8: purl.
Row 9: inc 1, K13, inc 2, K13, inc 1 [34 sts].
Row 10: purl.
Row 11: inc 1, K15, inc 2, K15, inc 1 [38 sts].
Row 12: purl.
Row 13: inc 1, K17, inc 2, K17, inc 1 [42 sts].
Row 14: purl.
Row 15: inc 1, K to last st, inc 1 [44 sts].
Row 16: purl.
Row 17: inc 1, K to last st, inc 1 [46 sts].
Row 18: purl.
Row 19: inc 1, K to last st, inc 1 [48 sts].
Row 20: purl.
Row 21: Cast off 16 sts knitwise, K to end [32 sts].
Row 22: Cast off 16 sts purlwise, P to end [16 sts].
Rows 23–30: beginning with a knit row, work st st.
Row 31: K1, *K1, K2tog*, rep from * to * to end [11 sts].
Row 32: purl.
Row 33: K1, *K2tog*, rep from * to * to end [6 sts].
Cut yarn, thread trailing end through remaining sts.

Adult male mallard

RIGHT WING (MAKE ONE)

Worked in st st. Using 4mm (UK 8, US 6) needles and light brown yarn, cast on 4 sts.

Row 1: inc 1, K2, inc 1 [6 sts].

Row 2: purl.

Row 3: inc 1, K4, inc 1 [8 sts].

Row 4: purl.

Row 5: inc 1, K6, inc 1 [10 sts].

Rows 6–8: beginning with a purl row, work st st.

Row 9: K to last 3 sts, K2tog, K1 [9 sts].

Row 10: purl.

Row 11: K to last 3 sts, K2tog, K1 [8 sts].

Row 12: purl.

Row 13: (light brown) K2, (dark blue) K3, (light brown) K2tog, K1 [7 sts].

Row 14: purl, keeping colour sequence.

Work in light brown only from now until the end of the wing.

Row 15: K to last 3 sts, K2tog, K1 [6 sts].

Row 16: purl.

Row 17: K to last 3 sts, K2tog, K1 [5 sts].

Row 18: purl.

Row 19: K2tog, K1, K2tog [3 sts].

Row 20: purl.

Cast off remaining sts.

LEFT WING (MAKE ONE)

Worked in st st. Using 4mm (UK 8, US 6) needles and light brown yarn, cast on 4 sts.

Row 1–8: work as for right wing.

Row 9: K1, K2tog, K to end [9 sts].

Row 10: purl.

Row 11: K1, K2tog, K to end [8 sts].

Row 12: purl.

Row 13: (light brown) K1, K2tog, (dark blue) K3, (light brown) K2 [7 sts].

Row 14: purl, keeping colour sequence.

Work in light brown only from now until the end of the wing.

Row 15: K1, K2tog, K to end [6 sts].

Row 16: purl.

Row 17: K1, K2tog, K to end [5 sts].

Row 18: purl.

Row 19: K2tog, K1, K2tog [3 sts].

Row 20: purl.

Cast off remaining sts.

MAKING UP

Follow the making up instructions for the male mallard (see page 19), using brown felt in place of the yellow for the beak, and sewing it to the head using brown thread.

Before sewing the wings into position, use cream yarn to sew a vertical stripe on either side of the blue wing flashes. Use a darning needle to sew the wings into place with the blue wing flashes near the end of the wing as shown below.

Adult female mallard

Male mallard's tail

Female mallard's wing flash

MALLARD DUCKLING

Materials

- Small amounts of 8-ply (DK) yarn in dark brown and yellow
- Two black seed beads
- Small amount of dark brown felt and matching cotton thread
- Black cotton thread and sewing needle
- Glass pebble
- Toy stuffing

Needles

- 4mm (UK 8, US 6) knitting needles

Tension

- 6 sts and 7 rows per 2.5cm (1in)

Size

- 6cm (2½in) from tip of beak to end of tail, 4cm (1½in) tall

Mallard duckling

Duckling bill template

BODY AND HEAD (MAKE ONE)

Worked in st st. Using 4mm (UK 8, US 6) needles and brown yarn, cast on 4 sts.

Row 1: K1, inc 2, K1 [6 sts].

Row 2: purl.

Row 3: K1, inc 1, K2, inc 1, K1 [8 sts].

Row 4: purl.

Row 5: *inc 1, K2, inc 1*, rep from * to * to end [12 sts].

Rows 6–10: beginning with a purl row, work st st.

Row 11: Using brown, cast on 4 sts at beginning of row, then (brown) K3, (yellow) K13 [16 sts].

From row 12 onwards, work with two balls of brown yarn.

Row 12: Using the second ball of brown, cast on 4 sts at beginning of row, then (brown) P3, (yellow) P14, (brown) P3 [20 sts].

Row 13: (brown) K2, (yellow) K6, K2tog, K2tog, K6, (brown) K2 [18 sts].

Row 14: purl, keeping colour sequence.

Row 15: (brown) K2, (yellow) K5, K2tog, K2tog, K5, (brown) K2 [16 sts].

Row 16: purl, keeping colour sequence.

Cast off, keeping colour sequence.

WINGS (MAKE TWO)

Worked in st st. Using 4mm (UK 8, US 6) needles and brown yarn, cast on 4 sts.

Row 1: knit.

Row 2: purl.

Row 3: Change to yellow, K2, (brown) K2.

Row 4: Change to brown, purl.

Row 5: K2, change to yellow, K2.

Row 6: Change to brown, purl.

Row 7: K1, K2tog, K1 [3 sts].

Row 8: P2tog, P1 [2 sts].

Cast off.

MAKING UP

Sew up the seam from the tail to where you cast on stitches to make the head. Stuff the body, including a glass pebble to give the duckling stability. Sew up the yellow chest seam, adding a little more stuffing if needed. Sew up the seam all round the head. Run a piece of yellow yarn around the neck and pull tight to create a distinction between the head and the body. Tie a knot and sew in the ends of the yarn.

Sew the wings into position. Cut out two pieces of brown felt for the beak, using the template. Sew the two pieces together along the dotted line on the template, using brown cotton and then sew the beak onto the head using brown cotton. Sew two beads onto the head for eyes, using black cotton. Sew a yellow stripe over each eye, using yellow yarn.

SONG THRUSH

The song thrush is a rather secretive bird with an incredibly loud and beautiful song.
If you see a stone in your garden surrounded by broken snail shells, you may well
have had a song thrush using it to break open its lunch.

Materials

- 20g (¾oz) medium brown 8-ply (DK) yarn (tail, back and wings)
- 10g (⅓oz) light brown 8-ply (DK) yarn (belly)
- Small amounts of dark brown 8-ply (DK) yarn (belly markings)
- Dark brown felt and matching cotton thread
- Two 5mm (¼in) black beads
- Black cotton thread and sewing needle
- One chenille stem and sticky tape
- 60cm (23½in) 28 gauge copper wire
- Salmon pink thread to wrap feet
- Toy stuffing

Needles

- 4mm (UK 8, US 6) knitting needles

Tension

- 6 sts and 7 rows per 2.5cm (1in)

Size

- 18cm (7in) long including beak, 10cm (4in) tall

NOTES

The pattern contains notes on working with two balls of yarn
for certain sections. Doing so makes your working easier
because you do not have to carry the yarn across the back of
the section.

The colours in parentheses indicate the yarn you should
use for the stitches that follow.

The thrush's tail contains a chenille stem for support.

BODY (MAKE ONE)

Worked in st st. Using 4mm (UK 8, US 6) needles and medium
brown yarn, cast on 8 sts.

Rows 1–16: beginning with a knit row, work st st.

Row 17: *inc 1, K2, inc 1*, rep from * to * to end of row
[12 sts].

Row 18: purl.

From row 19 onwards, work with two balls of each yarn.

Row 19: (light brown) inc 1, K3, (medium brown) K1, inc 2,
K1, (light brown) K3, inc 1 [16 sts].

Row 20: purl, keeping colour sequence.

Row 21: (light brown) inc 1, K5, (medium brown) K1, inc 2,
K1, (light brown) K5, inc 1 [20 sts].

Row 22: purl, keeping colour sequence.

Row 23: (light brown) inc 1, K7, (medium brown) K1, inc 2,
K1, (light brown) K7, inc 1 [24 sts].

Row 24: purl, keeping colour sequence.

Row 25: (light brown) inc 1, K9, (medium brown) K1, inc 2,
K1, (light brown) K9, inc 1 [28 sts].

Row 26: purl, keeping colour sequence.

Row 27: (light brown) K1, inc 1, K9, (medium brown) K6,
(light brown) K9, inc 1, K1 [30 sts].

Row 28: purl, keeping colour sequence.

Row 29: (light brown) K1, inc 1, K10, (medium brown) K6,
(light brown) K10, inc 1, K1 [32 sts].

Rows 30–38: beginning with a purl row, work st st, keeping
the colour sequence throughout.

Row 39: (light brown) K1, K2tog, K10, (medium brown) K6,
(light brown) K10, K2tog, K1 [30 sts].

Row 40: purl, keeping colour sequence.

Row 41: (light brown) K1, K2tog, K9, (medium brown) K6,
(light brown) K9, K2tog, K1 [28 sts].

Row 42: purl, keeping colour sequence.

Row 43: (light brown) K1, K2tog, K8, (medium brown) K6,
(light brown) K8, K2tog, K1 [26 sts].

Row 44: purl, keeping colour sequence.
Row 45: (light brown) K1, K2tog, K7, (medium brown) K6, (light brown) K7, K2tog, K1 [24 sts].
Row 46: purl, keeping colour sequence.
Row 47: (light brown) K1, K2tog, K6, (medium brown) K6, (light brown) K6, K2tog, K1 [22 sts].
Row 48: purl, keeping colour sequence.
Cast off, keeping colour sequence.

HEAD (MAKE ONE)
Worked in st st. Use two balls of light brown yarn when knitting the head. Using 4mm (UK 8, US 6) needles and light brown yarn, cast on 18 sts.
Row 1: (light brown) K6, (medium brown) K6, (light brown) K6.
Row 2: purl, keeping colour sequence.
Row 3: (light brown) K6, (medium brown) K6, (light brown) K6.
Row 4: purl, keeping colour sequence.
Row 5: (light brown) K6, (medium brown) K6, (light brown) K6.
Row 6: purl, keeping colour sequence.
Row 7: (light brown) K5, (medium brown) K8, (light brown) K5.
Row 8: (light brown) P4, (medium brown) P10, (light brown) P4.

Work in medium brown from this point to the end of the head.

Row 9: K2tog to end [9 sts].

Row 10: purl.

Row 11: K1, *K2tog*, rep from * to * to end [5 sts].

Cut yarn, thread tail through remaining sts.

WINGS (MAKE TWO)

Worked in st st. Using 4mm (UK 8, US 6) needles and medium brown yarn, cast on 4 sts.

Row 1: K1, inc 2, K1 [6 sts].

Row 2: purl.

Row 3: K1, inc 1, K2, inc 1, K1 [8 sts].

Row 4: purl.

Row 5: K1, inc 1, K4, inc 1, K1 [10 sts].

Row 6: purl.

Row 7: K1, inc 1, K6, inc 1, K1 [12 sts].

Row 8–20: beginning with a purl row, work st st.

Row 21: K1, K2tog, K to last 3 sts, K2tog, K1 [10 sts].

Row 22: purl.

Row 23: K1, K2tog, K to last 3 sts, K2tog, K1 [8 sts].

Row 24: purl.

Row 25: K1, K2tog, K to last 3 sts, K2tog, K1 [6 sts].

Row 26: purl.

Row 27: K1, K2tog, K2tog, K1 [4 sts].

Row 28: purl.

Row 29: K2tog to end [2 sts].

Row 30: purl.

Cast off.

MAKING UP

Sew up the body and tail seam, leaving a space in the belly to stuff. Do not sew up the end of the tail. Take a 15cm (6in) chenille stem, bend over 1cm (⅜in) at each end and secure with sticky tape so the ends are not sharp, then insert it into the length of the tail, with the rest of the chenille stem inside the body. Stuff the bird, making sure that the chenille stem in the body is surrounded by stuffing. Do not stuff the tail.

Sew up the belly seam. Sew up the seam at the end of the tail, pinching it first so that the tail lies flat. Sew up the head seam, stuff the head and sew it to the body using medium brown yarn to sew the back of the head and light brown yarn to match the body colour for the remainder. Attach the wings to the body.

Cut out two brown felt beak shapes using the template, then sew them together using brown thread and sew the beak to the head. Sew the two small black beads onto the head as eyes. Embroider spots on the chest using cross stitch and dark brown yarn.

Follow the posable legs instructions on page 15 to create legs using 60cm (23½in) of wire, wrapped with salmon pink thread.

Thrush beak template

Song thrush's cryptic chest markings

BLUE TIT

Cheeky and colourful, these tiny little birds brighten up a garden any time of year. Why not knit a flock of them and use their posable feet to attach them to a wire bird feeder?

> **NOTES**
> The colours in parentheses indicate the yarn you should use for the stitches that follow.

Materials

- Small amounts of 8-ply (DK) yarn in light yellow, light blue, cream, green and black
- Two 3mm (⅛in) black beads
- Small amount of black felt
- Black cotton thread and sewing needle
- 50cm (19¾in) 28 gauge black copper wire
- Black crochet cotton thread to wrap feet
- Toy stuffing

Needles

- 4mm (UK 8, US 6) knitting needles

Tension

- 6 sts and 7 rows per 2.5cm (1in)

Size

- 13cm (5in) from top of head to end of tail

BODY AND HEAD

Worked in st st. Using 4mm (UK 8, US 6) needles and light blue yarn, cast on 6 sts.

Rows 1–10: beginning with a knit row, work st st.

Row 11: inc 1, K4, inc 1 [8 sts].

Row 12: purl.

Row 13: (yellow) inc 1, K2, (green) inc 2, (yellow) K2, inc 1 [12 sts].

Row 14: purl, keeping colour sequence.

Row 15: (yellow) inc 1, K4, (green) inc 2, (yellow) K4, inc 1 [16 sts].

Row 16: purl, keeping colour sequence.

Row 17: (yellow) inc 1, K5, (green) K1, inc 2, K1 (yellow) K5, inc 1 [20 sts].

Row 18: purl, keeping colour sequence.

Row 19: (yellow) inc 1, K7, (green) K1, inc 2, K1 (yellow) K7, inc 1 [24 sts].

Rows 20–24: beginning with a purl row, work st st, keeping colour sequence.

Row 25: (yellow) K2tog, K7, (green) K6, (yellow) K7, K2tog [22sts].

Row 26: purl, keeping colour sequence.

Row 27: (yellow) K2tog, K6, (green) K6, (yellow) K6, K2tog [20 sts].

Row 28: purl, keeping colour sequence.

Row 29: (yellow) K2tog, K5, (green) K1, K2tog, K2tog, K1 (yellow) K5, K2tog [16 sts].

Change to cream.

Rows 30–35: beginning with a purl row, work st st.

Work in light blue from this point to the end.

Row 36: purl.

Row 37: K2tog to end [8 sts].

Row 38: purl.

Cut yarn, thread trailing end through remaining sts on needle.

WINGS (MAKE TWO)

Worked in st st. Using 4mm (UK 8, US 6) needles and light blue yarn, cast on 4 sts.

Row 1: inc 1, K2, inc 1 [6 sts].

Row 2: purl.

Row 3: inc 1, K4, inc 1 [8 sts].

Row 4: purl.

Row 5: inc 1, K6, inc 1 [10 sts].

Rows 6–10: beginning with a purl row, work st st.

Row 11: K1, K2tog, K4, K2tog, K1 [8 sts].

Row 12: purl.

Row 13: K1, K2tog, K2, K2tog, K1 [6 sts].

Row 14: purl.

Row 15: K1, K2tog, K2tog, K1 [4 sts].

Row 16: purl.

Row 17: K2tog to end [2 sts].

Row 18: purl.

Cast off remaining sts on needle.

MAKING UP INSTRUCTIONS

Pull the thread tight at the top of the head and sew up the seam from the head to halfway down the belly. Sew up the remainder of the belly and tail, stuffing the belly as you work but leaving the tail unstuffed. Sew up the end seam of the tail so that it lies flat.

Embroider black lines on the face using black crochet thread and sew on two black beads for eyes. Cut out a black felt beak using the template, fold it in half and sew up the seam using black cotton. Sew onto the bird using black cotton. Sew a line of cream yarn onto the wing, as shown in the pictures, then sew the wings onto the bird.

Follow the posable legs instructions on page 15 to create legs using 50cm (19¾in) of black copper wire, wrapped with black DK yarn.

Blue tit beak template

Blue tit's wing and back details

Blue tit's facial markings

30

CANADA GOOSE

Geese always seem to hate me. They will deliberately go out of their way to bother me. I even got chased across a field by some Canada geese that wanted my packet of crisps. Despite this, and to show that there are no hard feelings, I have included a Canada goose knitting pattern so you can knit a flock of your own.

Materials

- ❧ Small amounts of 8-ply (DK) yarn in black, cream, light brown and dark brown
- ❧ White and black felt
- ❧ Black and white cotton thread and needle
- ❧ Two 4mm (³⁄₁₆in) black beads
- ❧ One chenille stem and sticky tape
- ❧ Glass pebbles (for a goose without legs)
- ❧ Toy stuffing

For optional legs:
- ❧ 48cm (19in) of 18 gauge wire
- ❧ 15cm (6in) of 18 gauge wire
- ❧ Thin cardboard, such as from a cereal packet
- ❧ Two 25mm (1in) washers or small coins
- ❧ Strong white glue
- ❧ Sticky tape

Needles

- ❧ 4mm (UK 8, US 6) knitting needles

Tension

- ❧ 6 sts and 7 rows per 2.5cm (1in)

Size

- ❧ 12cm (4¾in) from front of body to tip of tail, 15cm (6in) tall excluding optional legs

NOTES ❧ ❧ ❧ ❧ ❧ ❧ ❧ ❧ ❧

The pattern contains notes on working with two balls of yarn for certain sections. Doing so makes your working easier because you do not have to carry the yarn across the back of the section.

The colours in parentheses indicate the yarn you should use for the stitches that follow.

BODY (MAKE ONE)

Worked in st st. Using 4mm (UK 8, US 6) needles and black yarn, cast on 16 sts. Work with two balls of cream yarn from this point.

Row 1: (cream) K4, (black) K8, (cream) K4.
Row 2: purl, keeping colour sequence.
Row 3: (cream) K4, (black) K8, (cream) K4.
Row 4: purl, keeping colour sequence.
Row 5: (cream) K4, (black) K8, (cream) K4.
Row 6: purl, keeping colour sequence.
Row 7: (cream) K4, (black) K8, (cream) K4.
Row 8: purl, keeping colour sequence.
Row 9: (cream) K4, (black) K8, (cream) K4.
Row 10: purl, keeping colour sequence.
Row 11: (cream) inc 1, K3, (light brown) K3, inc 2, K3, (cream) K3, inc 1 [20 sts].
Row 12: purl, keeping colour sequence.
Row 13: (cream) inc 1, K4, (light brown) K4, inc 2, K4, (cream) K4, inc 1 [24 sts].
Row 14: purl, keeping colour sequence.
Row 15: (cream) inc 1, K5, (light brown) K5, inc 2, K5, (cream) K5, inc 1 [28 sts].
Row 16: purl, keeping colour sequence.
Row 17: (cream) inc 1, K5, inc 1, (light brown) inc 1, K5, inc 2, K5, inc 1, (cream) inc 1, K5, inc 1 [36 sts].
Rows 18–22: beginning with a purl row, work st st, keeping the colour sequence.
Change to light brown yarn and work in this yarn from this point to the end of the body.
Rows 23–32: beginning with a knit row, work st st.
Row 33: *K2tog, K5, K2tog*, rep from * to * to end [28 sts].
Row 34: purl.
Row 35: K2tog, K to last 2 sts, K2tog [26 sts].
Row 36: P2tog, P to last 2 sts, P2tog [24 sts].
Row 37: K2tog, K to last 2 sts, K2tog [22 sts].
Cast off remaining sts on needle.

NECK AND HEAD (MAKE ONE)

Worked in st st. Using 4mm (UK 8, US 6) needles and light brown yarn, cast on 10 sts.

Rows 1–4: beginning with a knit row, work st st.

Change to black.

Rows 5–20: beginning with a knit row, work st st.

Row 21: K1, inc 1, K to last 2 sts, inc 1, K1 [12 sts].

Row 22: purl.

Row 23: K1, inc 1, K to last 2 sts, inc 1, K1 [14 sts].

Row 24: purl.

Row 25: K1, inc 2, K to last 3 sts, inc 2, K1 [18 sts].

Row 26: purl.

Row 27: K1, inc 2, K to last 3 sts, inc 2, K1 [22 sts].

Row 28: purl.

Row 29: K2tog to end [11 sts].

Row 30: purl.

Row 31: K1, *K2tog*, rep from * to * to end [6 sts].

Cut yarn, thread trailing end through remaining sts on needle.

LEFT WING (MAKE ONE)

Worked in st st. Using 4mm (UK 8, US 6) needles and dark brown yarn, cast on 4 sts.

Row 1: K1, inc 2, K1 [6 sts].

Row 2: purl.

Row 3: K1, inc 1, K2, inc 1, K1 [8 sts].

Row 4: purl.

Row 5: K1, inc 1, K4, inc 1, K1 [10 sts].

Row 6: purl.

Row 7: K1, inc 1, K6, inc 1, K1 [12 sts].

Row 8: purl.

Row 9: K1, inc 1, K8, inc 1, K1 [14 sts].

Row 10: purl.

Row 11: K1, K2tog, K to end of row [13 sts].

Row 12: purl.

Row 13: K1, K2tog, K to end of row [12 sts].

Row 14: purl.

Row 15: K1, K2tog, K to end of row [11 sts].

Row 16: purl.

Row 17: K1, K2tog, K to end of row [10 sts].

Row 18: purl.

Row 19: K1, K2tog, K to end of row [9 sts].

Row 20: purl.

Row 21: K1, K2tog, K to end of row [8 sts].

Row 22: purl.

Row 23: K1, K2tog, K to end of row [7 sts].

Row 24: purl.

Row 25: K1, K2tog, K to end of row [6 sts].

Row 26: purl.

Row 27: K1, K2tog, K to end of row [5 sts].

Row 28: purl.

Row 29: K1, K2tog, K to end of row [4 sts].

Row 30: purl.

Row 31: K2tog to end [2 sts].

Cast off remaining sts.

34

RIGHT WING (MAKE ONE)

Worked in st st. Using 4mm (UK 8, US 6) needles and dark brown yarn, cast on 4 sts.

Row 1–10: Work as for left wing.
Row 11: K11, K2tog, K1 [13 sts].
Row 12: purl.
Row 13: K10, K2tog, K1 [12 sts].
Row 14: purl.
Row 15: K9, K2tog, K1 [11 sts].
Row 16: purl.
Row 17: K8, K2tog, K1 [10 sts].
Row 18: purl.
Row 19: K7, K2tog, K1 [9 sts].
Row 20: purl.
Row 21: K6, K2tog, K1 [8 sts].
Row 22: purl.
Row 23: K5, K2tog, K1 [7 sts].
Row 24: purl.
Row 25: K4, K2tog, K1 [6 sts].
Row 26: purl.
Row 27: K3, K2tog, K1 [5 sts].
Row 28: purl.
Row 29: K2, K2tog, K1 [4 sts].
Row 30: purl.
Row 31: K2tog to end [2 sts].
Cast off remaining sts.

Canada goose templates

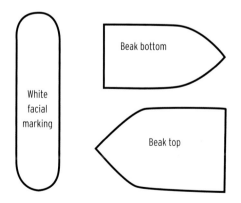

White facial marking

Beak bottom

Beak top

MAKING UP

Fold the body in half. Your cast-off stitches will form the bird's chest. Sew up this seam, then sew up the body and tail seam, leaving a space in the belly to allow you to add filling. Do not sew up the end of the tail.

If you are making a goose without legs, insert three or four glass pebbles into the belly to give the base a little weight – this will give your goose stability. Make sure that there is a thin layer of stuffing between the glass pebbles and the knitted fabric so that they are not visible. When you are happy with your pebbles and your stuffing, sew up the belly. If you are making a goose with legs, sew up the belly without inserting any pebbles – just add toy filling.

Sew up the seam at the end of the tail, using black yarn, pinching it first so that the tail lies flat. Take a chenille stem, bend over 1cm (½in) at one end and secure with sticky tape so that the end is not sharp. Wrap a little polyester stuffing around the chenille stem, then insert it into into the head to create the head shaping. Sew up the head seam and then sew up the neck, adding a tiny amount of polyester stuffing as you go to bulk out the neck. When you have sewn up the seam, trim the chenille stem so that 2.5cm (1in) is sticking out of the base of the neck – poke this length into the goose body to keep the neck stable and then sew the neck into position using brown body yarn. Sew the wings on to the body, with the long, flat side of the wing facing to the top.

Cut out the white felt face using the template and sew or glue it onto the head. Cut out two beak pieces from black felt, using the templates. Sew the side seams of the beak pieces using black cotton, stuff with a tiny amount of polyester stuffing and then sew onto the head. Sew two black beads onto the head for eyes.

For the optional legs, use a 48cm (19in) piece of 18 gauge wire and follow the supporting legs instructions on page 16 to make two legs, each approximately 3.75cm (1½in) long. Instead of toes, wrap the wire in a loose triangle with sides approximately 3.75cm (1½in) inches in length. Cut out a piece of thin cardboard to fit inside the triangle and use a coin or washer to add weight (see detail below). Once you have made and weighted the feet as described, wrap the legs in black 8-ply (DK) yarn and cover the feet with black felt.

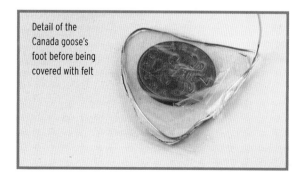

Detail of the Canada goose's foot before being covered with felt

BLACKBIRDS

The shiny, glossy blackbird has a beautiful ring around his eye and a brightly-coloured beak which contrasts against his black plumage. Female blackbirds are brown, but confusingly still called blackbirds. If you would like to knit your blackbird a partner, follow the same pattern using brown yarn instead of black.

The fledgling is modelled on a mournful-looking individual who appeared in my front garden one year. (I followed the RSPB's advice of leaving fledglings alone and eventually he happily flew off).

ADULT BLACKBIRD

NOTES
The blackbird's tail contains a chenille stem for support.

Materials
- 20g (¾oz) black 8-ply (DK) yarn
- Yellow felt and matching cotton thread
- Two 3mm (⅛in) black beads
- Black cotton thread and sewing needle
- One chenille stem and sticky tape
- 60cm (23½in) 28 gauge copper wire
- Black crochet cotton thread to wrap feet
- Toy stuffing

Needles
- 4mm (UK 8, US 6) knitting needles

Tension
- 6 sts and 7 rows per 2.5cm (1in)

Size
- 18cm (7in) long from tip of beak to end of tail

BODY (MAKE ONE)
Worked in st st. Using 4mm (UK 8, US 6) needles and black yarn, cast on 8 sts. Start knitting at the tail end.
Rows 1–20: Beginning with a knit row, work st st.
Row 21: *inc 1, K2, inc 1*, rep from * to * to end [12 sts].
Row 22: purl.
Row 23: *inc 1, K4, inc 1*, rep from * to * to end [16 sts].
Row 24: purl.
Row 25: *inc 1, K6, inc 1*, rep from * to * to end [20 sts].
Row 26: purl.
Row 27: *inc 1, K8, inc 1*, rep from * to * to end [24 sts].
Row 28: purl.
Row 29: *inc 1, K10, inc 1*, rep from * to * to end [28 sts].
Row 30: purl.
Row 31: K1, inc 1, K to last 2 sts, inc 1, K1 [30 sts].
Row 32: purl.
Row 33: K1, inc 1, K to last 2 sts, inc 1, K1 [32 sts].
Rows 34–42: beginning with a purl row, work st st.
Row 43: K1, K2tog, K to last 3 sts, K2tog, K1 [30 sts].
Row 44: purl.
Row 45: K1, K2tog, K to last 3 sts, K2tog, K1 [28 sts].
Row 46: purl.
Row 47: K1, K2tog, K to last 3 sts, K2tog, K1 [26 sts].
Row 48: purl.
Row 49: K1, K2tog, K to last 3 sts, K2tog, K1 [24 sts].
Row 50: purl.
Row 51: K1, K2tog, K to last 3 sts, K2tog, K1 [22 sts].
Row 52: purl.
Cast off remaining 22 sts.

Blackbird's tail

Blackbird beak template

HEAD (MAKE ONE)

Worked in st st. Using 4mm (UK 8, US 6) needles and black yarn, cast on 18 sts.

Rows 1–8: Beginning with a knit row, work st st.

Row 9: K2tog to end [9 sts].

Row 10: purl.

Row 11: K1, *K2tog, rep from * to end [5 sts].

Cut yarn, thread trailing end through remaining sts on needle.

WINGS (MAKE TWO, BOTH THE SAME)

Worked in st st. Using 4mm (UK 8, US 6) needles and black yarn, cast on 4 sts.

Row 1: K1, inc in next 2 sts, K1 [6 sts].

Row 2: purl.

Row 3: K1, inc 1, K to last 2 sts, inc 1, K1 [8 sts].

Row 4: purl.

Row 5: K1, inc 1, K to last 2 sts, inc 1, K1 [10 sts].

Row 6: purl.

Row 7: K1, inc 1, K to last 2 sts, inc 1, K1 [12 sts].

Rows 8–16: beginning with a purl row, work st st.

Row 17: K1, K2tog, K to last 3 sts, K2tog, K1 [10 sts].

Row 18: purl.

Row 19: K1, K2tog, K to last 3 sts, K2tog, K1 [8 sts].

Row 20: purl.

Row 21: K1, K2tog, K to last 3 sts, K2tog, K1 [6 sts].

Row 22: purl.

Row 23: K1, K2tog, K2tog, K1 [4 sts].

Row 24: purl.

Row 25: K2tog to end [2 sts].

Row 26: purl.

Cast off remaining 2 sts.

MAKING UP

Sew up the body and tail seam, leaving a space in the belly to stuff. Do not sew up the end of the tail. Take a 15cm (6in) length of chenille stem, bend over 1cm (⅜in) at each end and secure with sticky tape so that the ends are not sharp, then insert into the length of the tail, with the rest of the chenille stem inside the body. Stuff the bird's body, making sure that the end of the chenille stem is surrounded by stuffing. Do not stuff the tail. Sew up the belly seam. Sew up the seam at the end of the tail, pinching it first so that the tail lies flat.

Sew up the head seam, stuff the head and then attach it to the body. Sew the wings to the body. Cut out two yellow felt beak shapes using the template, overstitch together using yellow thread, leaving open the end that will be attached to the head. Sew to the head. Cut out two yellow felt circles, 7mm (¼in) across and sew a small black bead into the middle of each of these using black cotton thread, and then sew on to the head for eyes.

Follow the posable legs instruction on page 15 to create legs using 60cm (23½in) of black copper wire, wrapped with black crochet cotton.

FLEDGLING BLACKBIRD

Materials

- 10g (⅓oz) brown 8-ply (DK) yarn
- 5g (⅛oz) black lace weight (superfine) mohair/silk mix yarn
- Two 5mm (¼in) black beads
- Black cotton thread and sewing needle
- Pale brown felt
- Light brown cotton thread to match felt
- Two or three glass pebbles
- Toy stuffing

Needles

- 4mm (UK 8, US 6) knitting needles

Tension

- 4.5 sts and 6.5 rows per 2.5cm (1in)

Size

- 9cm (3½in) tall

NOTES

Work with brown 8-ply (DK) yarn and black laceweight (superfine) mohair together throughout. The mohair gives a downy, baby feather effect to the fledgling.

HEAD AND BODY (MAKE ONE)

Worked in st st. Using 4mm (UK 8, US 6) needles and brown and black worked together, cast on 8 sts.
Row 1: *inc 1, K2, inc 1*, rep from * to * to end [12 sts].
Row 2: purl.
Row 3: *inc 1, K4, inc 1*, rep from * to * to end [16 sts].
Row 4: purl.
Row 5: *inc 1, K6, inc 1*, rep from * to * to end [20 sts].
Row 6: purl.
Row 7: *inc 1, K8, inc 1*, rep from * to * to end [24 sts].
Row 8: purl.
Row 9: *inc 1, K10, inc 1*, rep from * to * to end [28 sts].
Rows 10-16: beginning with a purl row, work st st.
Row 17: K2tog, K to last 2 sts, K2tog [26 sts].
Row 18: purl.
Row 19: K2tog, K to last 2 sts, K2tog [24 sts].
Row 20: purl.
Row 21: Cast off 4 sts knitwise, K to end [20 sts].
Row 22: Cast off 4 sts purlwise, P to end [16 sts].
Rows 23-26: beginning with a knit row, work st st.

Row 27: K2tog to end [8 sts].
Row 28: purl.
Row 29: K2tog to end [4 sts].
Cut yarn, thread trailing end through remaining sts on needle.

WINGS (MAKE TWO)

Worked in st st. Using 4mm (UK 8, US 6) needles and brown and black worked together, cast on 5 sts.
Row 1-6: beginning with a knit row, work st st.
Row 7: K2tog, K1, K2tog [3 sts].
Row 8: purl.
Row 9: K2tog, K1 [2 sts].
Cast off remaining sts.

TAIL (MAKE ONE)

Worked in st st. Using 4mm (UK 8, US 6) needles and brown and black worked together, cast on 8 sts.
Rows 1-10: beginning with a knit row, work st st.
Cast off remaining sts.

MAKING UP

Sew up the head and body seam, starting at the head. Start stuffing when you have sewn up approximately three-quarters of the seam, then insert two or three glass pebbles to weigh the base of the fledgling down and help to give it stability. Tuck stuffing all around the pebbles so that they do not poke through the knitted fabric surface. Sew up the remaining head and body seam and when the bird is stuffed to your liking, sew up the bottom seam.

Use the templates to cut out the two pieces of the beak from light brown felt. Position the beak bottom under the beak top then use light brown thread to overstitch the two pieces together along the dotted line marked on the template. Sew the beak onto position on the head, making sure that the ends of the beak are turned down slightly to give a forlorn look!

Cut out two circles of light brown felt which are slightly larger than your beads. Position these circles on the head where you want the eyes to go, and then sew a black bead on top of each, using black thread. Sew the wings into position on the sides of the body. Sew up the long tail seam, flatten the tail so that it lies flat with the long seam underneath, and then sew up the seam at the tip of the tail. Sew the tail onto the body, with the long seam underneath.

Fledgling beak templates

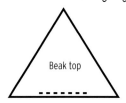

Beak top

Beak bottom

Blackbird fledgling's eyes and beak

MUTE SWANS

Swans are graceful and majestic – the royalty of the river. Smaller water birds respect swans and move out of their way, so this little family of knitted mute swans out for a swim will probably be first in line for any bread that you happen to have on you.

Materials
- 30g (1oz) cream 8-ply (DK) yarn
- Five or six glass pebbles
- Small amount of orange felt and matching cotton thread
- Small amount of black felt
- Black cotton thread and sewing needle
- Two 3mm (⅛in) black beads
- Chenille stem and sticky tape
- Toy stuffing

Needles
- 4mm (UK 8, US 6) knitting needles

Tension
- 6 sts and 7 rows per 2.5cm (1in)

Size
- 18cm (7in) long, 16.5cm (6½in) tall

ADULT SWAN

BODY AND HEAD (MAKE ONE)

Worked in st st. Using 4mm (UK 8, US 6) needles and cream yarn, cast on 8 sts.

Row 1: *inc 1, K2, inc 1*, rep from * to * to end [12 sts].
Row 2: purl.
Row 3: *inc 1, K4, inc 1*, rep from * to * to end [16 sts].
Row 4: purl.
Row 5: *inc 1, K6, inc 1*, rep from * to * to end [20 sts].
Row 6: purl.
Row 7: *inc 1, K8, inc 1*, rep from * to * to end [24 sts].
Row 8: purl.
Row 9: *inc 1, K10, inc 1*, rep from * to * to end [28 sts].
Row 10: purl.
Row 11: *inc 1, K5, inc 1*, rep from * to * to end [36 sts].
Row 12: purl.
Row 13: *inc 1, K7, inc 1*, rep from * to * to end [44 sts].
Rows 14–36: beginning with a purl row, work st st.
Row 37: *K2tog, K7, K2tog*, rep from * to * to end [36 sts].
Row 38: purl.
Row 39: *K2tog, K5, K2tog*, rep from * to * to end [28 sts].
Row 40: purl.
Row 41: *K2tog, K10, K2tog*, rep from * to * to end [24 sts].
Row 42: purl.
Row 43: *K2tog, K8, K2tog*, rep from * to * to end [20 sts].
Row 44: purl.
Row 45: *K2tog, K6, K2tog*, rep from * to * to end [16 sts].
Row 46: purl.
Row 47: *K2tog, K4, K2tog*, rep from * to * to end [12 sts].
Rows 48–76: beginning with a purl row, work st st.
Row 77: K1, inc 2, K6, inc 2, K1 [16 sts].
Row 78: purl.
Row 79: K1, inc 2, K10, inc 2, K1 [20 sts].
Rows 80–84: beginning with a purl row, work st st.
Row 85: K2tog to end [10 sts].
Row 86: purl.
Row 87: K2tog to end [5 sts].

Cut yarn, thread trailing end through remaining sts on needle.

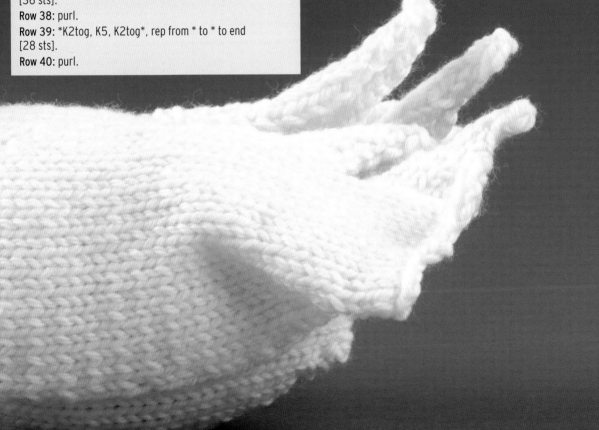

LEFT WING (MAKE ONE)

Worked in st st. Using 4mm (UK 8, US 6) needles and cream yarn, cast on 4 sts.

Row 1: K1, inc 2, K1 [6 sts].
Row 2: purl.
Row 3: K1, inc 1, K2, inc 1, K1 [8 sts].
Row 4: purl.
Row 5: K1, inc 1, K4, inc 1, K1 [10 sts].
Row 6: purl.
Row 7: K1, inc 1, K6, inc 1, K1 [12 sts].
Row 8: purl.
Row 9: K1, inc 1, K8, inc 1, K1 [14 sts].
Row 10: purl.
Row 11: K1, inc 1, K10, inc 1, K1 [16 sts].
Row 12: purl.
Row 13: K14, inc 1, K1 [17 sts].
Row 14: purl.
Row 15: K15, inc 1, K1 [18 sts].
Rows 16–34: beginning with a purl row, work st st.
Row 35: K1, K2tog, K to end [17 sts].
Row 36: purl.
Begin lower feather shaping
Row 37: cast off 4 sts, K to end [13 sts].
Rows 38–40: beginning with a purl row, work st st.
Row 41: K1, K2tog, K to end [12 sts].
Rows 42–44: beginning with a purl row, work st st.
Row 45: cast off 4 sts, K to end [8 sts].
Row 46: purl.
Row 47: K1, K2tog, K2, K2tog, K1 [6 sts].
Row 48: purl.
Row 49: K1, K2tog, K2tog, K1 [4 sts].
Row 50: purl.
Row 51: K1, K2tog, K1 [3 sts].
Cast off remaining sts.

RIGHT WING (MAKE ONE)

Worked in st st. Using 4mm (UK 8, US 6) needles and cream yarn, cast on 4 sts.

Rows 1–12: work as for the left wing [16 sts].
Row 13: K1, inc 1, K to end [17 sts].
Row 14: purl.
Row 15: K1, inc 1, K to end [18 sts].
Rows 16–34: beginning with a purl row, work st st.
Row 35: K to last 3 sts, K2tog, K1 [17 sts].
Row 36: purl.
Row 37: knit.
Begin lower feather shaping.

Row 38: cast off 4 sts purlwise, P to end [13 sts].
Row 39: knit.
Row 40: purl.
Row 41: K10, K2tog, K1 [12 sts].
Row 42–45: beginning with a purl row, work st st.
Row 46: cast off 4 sts purlwise, P to end [8 sts].
Row 47: K1, K2tog, K2, K2tog, K1 [6 sts].
Row 48: purl.
Row 49: K1, K2tog, K2tog, K1 [4 sts].
Row 50: purl.
Row 51: K1, K2tog, K1 [3 sts].
Cast off remaining sts.

WING FEATHERS (MAKE FOUR)

Worked in st st. Using 4mm (UK 8, US 6) needles and cream yarn, cast on 8 sts.

Rows 1–16: beginning with a knit row, work st st.
Row 17: K1, K2tog, K2, K2tog, K1 [6 sts].
Row 18–20: beginning with a purl row, work st st.
Row 21: K1, K2tog, K2tog, K1 [4 sts].
Row 22: purl.
Row 23: K1, K2tog, K1 [3 sts].
Cast off remaining sts.

MAKING UP

Sew up the body seam, starting at the tail end and stuffing as you go. Stop before you get to the neck.

Bend over a 15cm (6in) chenille stem 1cm (⅜in) from the end and secure with sticky tape so the end is not sharp, then insert it into the head, wrapping a little polyester stuffing around the chenille stem to create the head shaping. Sew up the head seam and then sew up the neck, adding a little polyester stuffing as you go to bulk out the neck. Do not overstuff, and ensure that the sharp end of the chenille stem is surrounded by body stuffing so that it does not poke out.

Insert five or six glass pebbles into the base of the swan body to give it some stability. Make sure that there is a thin layer of stuffing between the glass pebbles and the knitted fabric so that they are not visible. When you are happy with your pebbles and your stuffing, sew up the entire body seam. The neck and head will probably be flopping forward – secure the base of the neck to the upper body with a few stitches.

Using the picture for reference, pin the wings into position with the straight edge towards the top of the body and the lower feather shaping towards the bottom. Next, pin two feathers behind each wing, with 2.5–5cm (1–2in) protruding as shown. Sew the feathers into place, then sew the wings to the body, leaving free both the shaping at the tail end of the wing and the part where you have placed the feathers.

Cut out the two bill pieces from orange felt, using the templates below. Sew the two pieces together, using orange thread, and leave the end open that will be attached to the head. Stuff lightly with a little polyester stuffing and sew into position on the head.

Cut out the black face shape, using the template and black felt. You may need to trim it slightly to best fit your bird's face as the shape will vary slightly depending on how much stuffing was used. Sew it into position using black thread.

Cut out the black bill top shape, using the template and black felt. Sew this into position at the top of the bill, using black thread. To finish, sew two beads onto the head, for eyes, using black thread.

Adult mute swan's facial markings

Adult mute swan's neck

Mute swan templates

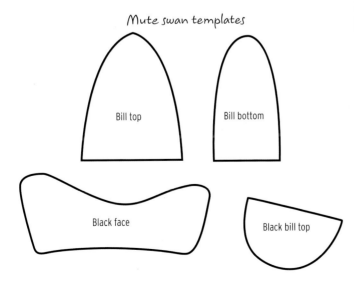

Bill top

Bill bottom

Black face

Black bill top

43

CYGNET

NOTES
Work the light grey and mohair yarns together throughout – the addition of the mohair helps to creates a fluffy, downy texture.

Materials

- Small amount of light grey 8-ply (DK) yarn
- Small amounts of cream laceweight (superfine) mohair/silk mix yarn
- Chenille stem and sticky tape
- Two or three glass pebbles
- Small amount of black felt
- Black cotton thread and sewing needle
- Two 2mm (1/16in) black beads
- Toy stuffing

Needles

- 4mm (UK 8, US 6) knitting needles

Tension

- 5 sts and 7 rows per 2.5cm (1in)

Size

- 6.5cm (2½n) long, 7.5cm (3in) tall

BODY, NECK AND HEAD (MAKE ONE)

Worked in st st. Using 4mm (UK 8, US 6) needles and grey and mohair yarn worked together, cast on 8 sts.

Row 1: *inc 1, K2, inc 1*, rep from * to * to end [12 sts].
Row 2: purl.
Row 3: *inc 1, K4, inc 1*, rep from * to * to end [16 sts].
Row 4: purl.
Row 5: *inc 1, K6, inc 1*, rep from * to * to end [20 sts].
Rows 6–10: beginning with a purl row, work st st.
Row 11: *K2tog, K6, K2tog*, rep from * to * to end [16 sts].
Row 12: purl.
Row 13: *K2tog, K4, K2tog*, rep from * to * to end [12 sts].
Row 14: purl.
Row 15: *K2tog, K2, K2tog*, rep from * to * to end [8 sts].
Row 16: purl.
Row 17: K2, K2tog, K2tog, K2 [6 sts].
Rows 18–26: beginning with a purl row, work st st.
Row 27: K1, inc 1, K2, inc 1, K1 [8 sts].
Rows 28–30: beginning with a purl row, work st st.
Row 31: K2tog to end (4 sts).
Row 32: purl.
Run yarn through remaining sts.

WINGS (MAKE TWO)

Worked in st st. Using 4mm (UK 8, US 6) needles and grey and mohair yarn worked together, cast on 2 sts.

Row 1: inc 2 [4 sts].
Rows 2–6: beginning with a purl row, work st st.
Row 7: K1, K2tog, K1 [3 sts].
Row 8: P1, P2tog [2 sts].
Cast off remaining sts on needle.

Cygnet beak template

MAKING UP

Sew up the body seam, starting at the tail end and stuffing as you go. Insert glass pebbles into the base of the body to give the cygnet stability. Make sure that there is a thin layer of stuffing between the glass pebble and the knitted fabric so they are not visible. When you are happy with your pebble and your stuffing, sew up the body seam, stopping approximately 2cm (¾in) before you get to the neck.

Bend a chenille stem over 1cm (⅜in) from the end and secure with sticky tape so that the end is not sharp, then insert it into the head. Sew up the head seam and then sew up the neck. Note that there is no need to stuff the head and the neck. Make sure that the sharp end of the chenille stem ends up in the body, surrounded by body stuffing so that it does not poke out. Trim it off if necessary.

Sew the wings into position, then use the template and cut out the beak shape from black felt. Fold it in half along the dotted line on the template and sew the two sides together using black cotton thread. Sew the open end of the beak onto the head, using black cotton thread. To finish, sew two seed bead eyes into position on the sides of the head, using black cotton.

BARN OWLS

Barn owls glide through the night in total silence, like a ghost. If you are lucky enough to see one of these mysterious and elegant birds in flight, the image stays with you for a long time.

Barn owl babies, on the other hand, are cute, fluffy and rather ungainly. They will learn all the majestic gliding and mouse-catching skills as they get older.

Materials

- ↓ Small amounts of 8-ply (DK) yarn in cream, light brown, and light grey
- ↓ Black felt
- ↓ Very light brown felt and matching cotton thread (for face)
- ↓ Contrasting light brown felt and matching cotton thread (for beak)
- ↓ Black cotton thread and sewing needle
- ↓ Golden brown embroidery thread (to sew lines on face) and embroidery needle
- ↓ Four or five glass pebbles
- ↓ 4mm (UK 8, US G/6) crochet hook
- ↓ Toy stuffing

Needles

- ↓ 4mm (UK 8, US 6) knitting needles

Tension

- ↓ 6 sts and 7 rows per 2.5cm (1in)

Size

- ↓ 10cm (4in) wide, 11.5cm (4½in) tall

NOTES

The colours in parentheses indicate the yarn you should use for the stitches that follow.

ADULT BARN OWL

BODY AND HEAD (MAKE ONE)

Using 4mm (UK 8, US 6) needles and light brown, cast on 16 sts.

Row 1: *inc, K6, inc*, (cream) repeat from * to * to end [20 sts].

Row 2: purl, keeping colour sequence.

Row 3: (light brown) *inc, K3, inc*, rep from * to * once, then (cream) rep twice more to end [28 sts].

Row 4: purl, keeping colour sequence.

Row 5: (light brown) *inc, K5, inc*, rep from * to * once, then (cream) rep twice more to end [36 sts].

Row 6: purl, keeping colour sequence.

Row 7: (light brown) *inc, K7, inc*, rep from * to * once, then (cream) rep twice more to end [44 sts].

Rows 8–22: beginning with a purl row, work st st, keeping colour sequence.

Row 23: (light brown) *K2tog, K18, K2tog*, (cream) rep from * to * to end [40 sts].

Row 24: purl, keeping colour sequence.

Row 25: (light brown) *K2tog, K16, K2tog*, (cream) rep from * to * to end [36 sts].

Row 26: purl, keeping colour sequence.

Row 27: (light brown) *K2tog, K14, K2tog*, (cream) rep from * to * to end [32 sts].

Row 28: purl, keeping colour sequence.

Row 29: (light brown) *K2tog, K12, K2tog*, (cream) rep from * to * to end [28 sts].

Rows 30–38: (light brown) work 9 rows st st, starting and ending with a P row.

Row 39: K2tog to end [14 sts].

Row 40: purl.

Row 41: (K2tog) to end [7 sts].

Cut yarn, thread trailing end through remaining sts on needle.

WINGS (MAKE TWO)

Using 4mm (UK 8, US 6) needles and light brown and grey yarn worked together to create a speckled effect, cast on 4 sts.

Row 1: K1, inc 2, K1 [6 sts].

Row 2: purl.

Row 3: K1, inc 1, K2, inc 1, K1 [8 sts].

Row 4: purl.

Row 5: K1, inc 1, K4, inc 1, K1 [10 sts].

Rows 6–10: beginning with a purl row, work st st.

Row 11: K1, K2tog, K to last 3 sts, K2tog, K1 [8 sts].

Row 12: purl.

Row 13: K1, K2tog, K to last 3 sts, K2tog, K1 [6 sts].

Row 14: purl.

Row 15: K1, K2tog, K2tog, K1 [4 sts].

Row 16: purl.

Row 17: K2tog, K2tog [2 sts].

Row 18: P2tog [1 st].

Cut yarn, thread trailing end through remaining sts on needle.

MAKING UP

Sew up the side seam, starting at the head. Start stuffing the owl when you have sewn up approximately three-quarters of the side seam, then insert the glass pebbles to weigh the base of the owl down and help to give it stability. Tuck stuffing all around the pebbles so that they do not poke through the knitted fabric surface. Sew up the remaining side seam and when the bird is stuffed to your liking, sew up the bottom seam.

Using the template, cut out a face shape from light brown felt. Cut out two black felt eyes, using the template, and sew into position on the felt face using black thread. Cut out a beak from contrasting brown felt and sew it onto the face using matching thread (alternatively, the eyes and beak can be glued on).

Sew two lines of running stitch, using golden brown embroidery thread, round the eyes and down to the beak, using the pictures as reference. Next, sew the face onto the head using a cotton thread the same colour as the face felt.

Using a 4mm (UK 8, US G/6) crochet hook and the same yarn that you used for the body, create a crochet chain that is long enough to fit all the way round the edge of the face – approximately 18cm (7in). Sew the chain into position, using a cotton thread in the same colour as the face felt.

Position the wings, then sew the top third of each wing to the body, leaving the rest free.

Using grey 8-ply (DK) yarn, sew a scattering of Swiss darning stitches (see page 17) onto the owl's belly, as shown in the pictures, to finish.

Barn owl templates

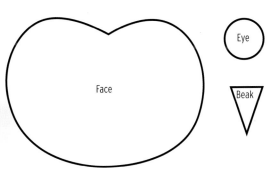

BARN OWLET

Materials

- Small amount of 8-ply (DK) yarn: cream
- Small amount of superfine mohair/silk mix yarn: cream
- Black felt (for eyes)
- Cream felt (for face)
- Light brown felt (for beak)
- Black cotton thread
- Cream cotton thread (to match face felt)
- Light brown cotton thread (to match beak felt)
- One or two glass pebbles
- 3.5mm (UK 9, US E/00) crochet hook
- Toy stuffing

Needles

- 4mm (UK 8, US 6) knitting needles

Tension

- 5 sts and 7 rows per 2.5cm (1in)

Size

- 6cm (2½in) wide, 8cm (3in) tall

Barn owlet's face

NOTES
Work the cream 8-ply (DK) and mohair/silk yarns together throughout, to create a fluffy, downy texture.

HEAD AND BODY (MAKE ONE)

Using 4mm (UK 8, US 6) needles and the two yarns worked together, cast on 8 sts.

Row 1: *inc, K2, inc*, repeat from * to * to end [12 sts].

Row 2: purl.

Row 3: *inc, K4, inc*, repeat from * to * to end [16 sts].

Row 4: purl.

Row 5: *inc, K6, inc*, repeat from * to * to end [20 sts].

Row 6: purl.

Row 7: *inc, K8, inc*, repeat from * to * to end [24 sts].

Rows 8–14: beginning with a purl row, work st st.

Row 15: *K2tog, K8, K2tog*, repeat from * to * to end [20 sts].

Row 16: purl.

Row 17: *K2tog, K6, K2tog*, repeat from * to * to end [16 sts].

Rows 18–22: beginning with a purl row, work st st.

Row 23: K2tog to end [8 sts].

Row 24: purl.

Row 25: K2tog to end [4 sts].

Cut yarn, thread trailing end through remaining sts on needle.

WINGS (MAKE TWO)

Using 4mm (UK 8, US 6) needles and the two yarns worked together, cast on 2 sts.

Row 1: inc into both sts [4 sts].

Rows 2–6: Beginning with a purl row, work st st.

Row 7: K1, K2tog, K1 [3 sts].

Row 8: purl.

Cast off remaining sts.

MAKING UP

Sew up the side seam, starting at the head. Start stuffing when you have sewn up approximately three-quarters of the side seam, then insert a glass pebble to weigh down the base of the owlet and help give it stability. Tuck stuffing all around the pebble so that it does not poke through the knitted fabric surface. Sew up the remaining side seam and when the bird is stuffed to your liking, sew up the bottom seam.

Using the template, cut out a face shape from cream felt. Cut out two black felt eyes, using the template, and sew them into position on the felt face using black thread. Cut out a beak from contrasting brown felt and sew onto face using matching thread (alternatively, both eyes and beak can be glued on). Sew the face onto the owlet's head, using a cotton thread in the same colour as the face felt.

Using a 3.5mm (UK 9, US E/00) crochet hook and a double length (i.e. working two strands together at the same time) of fluffy cream yarn, create a crochet chain that is long enough to fit all the way round the edge of the felt face – approximately 14cm (5½in). Sew the chain into position, using a cotton thread the same colour as the face felt.

Cut short lengths of cream mohair/silk blend yarn, each approximately 8–10cm (3⅛–4in) in length. Using the crochet hook, attach the lengths to the knitted fabric at random intervals around the face to create short tufts. Once attached, trim to varied lengths to create a straggly feathered effect. Finally, sew the wings into position to finish.

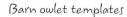

Barn owlet templates

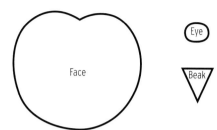

AVOCET

The avocet has a curved beak, which it uses to catch food in shallow water, moving its head from side to side as it walks. This big, beautiful knitted avocet has stiff wire legs and needs to be glued to a piece of driftwood or similar solid base.

NOTES

The avocet is mounted onto a piece of driftwood to give it stability. The piece I used measured 18 x 10cm (7 x 4in), but the exact size is not important. The crucial thing is that it is large and heavy enough to keep your avocet upright.

The colours in parentheses indicate the yarn you should use for the stitches that follow.

The pattern contains notes on working with two balls of yarn for certain sections. Doing so makes your working easier because you do not have to carry the yarn across the back of the section.

Materials

- 80g (2¾oz) of cream DK yarn
- Small amounts of black and grey 8-ply (DK) yarn
- 31cm (12in) chenille stem
- Two 5mm (¼in) black beads for eyes
- 90cm (35in) of 18 gauge craft wire for the legs
- 20cm (8in) length of 20 gauge craft wire for the beak
- Small amount of grey felt
- Pliers
- Sharp darning needle
- 5mm (UK 6, US H/8) crochet hook
- Toy stuffing
- Glue gun or craft glue
- A heavy piece of driftwood

Needles

- 4mm (UK 8, US 6) knitting needles

Tension

- 6 sts and 7 rows per 2.5cm (1in)

Size

- 24cm (9½in) long from head to tail, 30cm (11¾in) tall including legs

BODY AND HEAD (MAKE ONE)

Worked in st st. Using 4mm (UK 8, US 6) needles and cream cast on 8 sts.

Row 1: *inc 1, K2, inc 1*, rep from * to * to end of row [12 sts].

Row 2: purl.

Row 3: *inc 1, K4, inc 1*, rep from * to * to end of row [16 sts].

Row 4: purl.

Row 5: *inc 1, K6, inc 1*, rep from * to * to end of row [20 sts].

Row 6: purl.

Row 7: *inc 1, K8, inc 1*, rep from * to * to end of row [24 sts].

Row 8: purl.

Row 9: *inc 1, K10, inc 1*, rep from * to * to end of row [28 sts].

Row 10: purl.

Row 11: *inc 1, K5, inc 1*, rep from * to * to end of row [36 sts].

Rows 12–26: beginning with a purl row, work st st.

Row 27: K16, K2tog, K2tog, K16 [34 sts].
Row 28: purl.
Row 29: K15, K2tog, K2tog, K15 [32 sts].
Row 30: purl.
Row 31: K14, K2tog, K2tog, K14 [30 sts].
Row 32: purl.
Row 33: K13, K2tog, K2tog, K13 [28 sts].
Row 34: purl.
Row 35: K12, K2tog, K2tog, K12 [26 sts].
Row 36: purl.
Row 37: *K2tog, K9, K2tog*, rep from * to * to end of row [22 sts].
Row 38: purl.
Row 39: *K2tog, K7, K2tog*, rep from * to * to end of row [18 sts].
Row 40: purl.
Row 41: K7, K2tog, K2tog, K7 [16 sts].
Rows 42–46: beginning with a purl row, work st st.

From this point onwards, work with two balls of cream yarn.
Row 47: (cream) K6, (black) K4, (cream) K6.
Row 48: purl, keeping colour sequence.
Row 49: (cream) K6, (black) K4, (cream) K6.
Row 50: purl, keeping colour sequence.
Row 51: (cream) K6, (black) K4, (cream) K6.
Row 52: purl, keeping colour sequence.
Row 53: (cream) K6, (black) K4, (cream) K6.
Row 54: purl, keeping colour sequence.
Row 55: (cream) K6, (black) K4, (cream) K6.
Row 56: purl, keeping colour sequence.
Row 57: (cream) K1, inc 1, K4, (black) K4, (cream) K4, inc 1, K1 [18 sts].
Row 58: purl, keeping colour sequence.
Row 59: (cream) K1, inc 1, K5, (black) K4, (cream) K5, inc 1, K1 [20 sts].
Row 60: purl, keeping colour sequence.
Row 61: (cream) K1, inc 2, K5, (black) K4, (cream) K5, inc 2, K1 [24 sts].
Rows 62–64: beginning with a purl row, work st st, keeping colour sequence.
Work all in black from this point to the end of the head.
Rows 65–68: beginning with a knit row, work st st.
Row 69: *K1, K2tog*, rep from * to * to end [16 sts].
Row 70: purl.
Row 71: K2tog to end [8 sts].
Cut yarn, thread trailing end through remaining sts on needle.

WING (MAKE TWO)

Worked in st st. Using 4mm (UK 8, US 6) needles and cream yarn, cast on 4 sts.

Row 1: K1, inc 2, K1 [6 sts].
Row 2: purl.
Row 3: K1, inc 1, K2, inc 1, K1 [8 sts].
Row 4: purl.
Row 5: K1, inc 1, K4, inc 1, K1 [10 sts].
Row 6: purl.
Row 7: K1, inc 1, K6, inc 1, K1 [12 sts].
Row 8: purl.
Row 9: K1, inc 1, K8, inc 1, K1 [14 sts].
Row 10: purl.
Row 11: K1, inc 1, K10, inc 1, K1 [16 sts].
Rows 12-22: beginning with a purl row, work st st.
Row 23: K1, K2tog, K10, K2tog, K1 [14 sts].
Row 24: purl.
Row 25: K1, K2tog, K8, K2tog, K1 [12 sts].
Row 26: purl.
Row 27: K1, K2tog, K6, K2tog, K1 [10 sts].
Row 28: purl.
Row 29: K1, K2tog, K4, K2tog, K1 [8 sts].
Row 30: purl.
Row 31: K1, K2tog, K2, K2tog, K1 [6 sts].
Row 32: purl.
Row 33: K1, K2tog, K2tog, K1 [4 sts].
Row 34: purl.
Row 35: K2tog to end [2 sts].
Row 36: purl.
Cast off remaining sts on needle.

Detail of the avocet's foot, showing the felt webbing

MAKING UP

Sew up the body seam from the tail to 2.5cm (1in) before the neck decrease. Stuff. Fold a chenille stem in half and insert it into the head and neck, with the sharp end stuck into the body stuffing, and the folded end in the head. Sew up the seam from the top of the head to the base of the neck, lightly stuffing as you go. When you are happy with the stuffing, sew up the rest of the body seam.

Overstitch all the way round the edge of both wings using black yarn to give the wings a black border. To make the black curved stripe that runs horizontally across the wing, work a 10cm (4in) length of crochet chain stitch using black yarn and a 5mm (UK 6, US H/8) crochet hook. Measure the length against the wing to ensure a good fit. Sew the wing into position, using the pictures for reference, then repeat for the other wing.

To make the beak, take the 20cm (8in) length of 20 gauge craft wire and bend it in half. The sharp ends of wire will be inserted into the head. Bend the wire into the slight curve of the neck, using the pictures for reference. Starting at the sharp end, and leaving 1.5cm (¾in) unwrapped, wrap the beak with black 8-ply (DK) yarn. Thread a darning needle onto the yarn and wrap the yarn around both pieces of wire to bind them together, until you reach 1cm (½in) from the tip of the beak. Then, wrap the yarn around one piece of wire only, until you have worked your way all round the tip. This is the same technique as making a toe for posable legs (see page 15).

Next, squash the tip of the beak flat with pliers. When the beak is entirely wrapped apart from the 1.5cm (¾in), secure the yarn by weaving the end back though some of the wrapping using the darning needle.

Insert the unwrapped wire into the head and secure the beak to the head with black cotton, making sure that the cotton is sewn through your wool wrapping in several places to keep the beak stable. Sew two black beads on to the head for eyes, using black cotton.

You will need a piece of wire at least 86cm (34in) long to make the legs. Work with a longer piece until you have the legs formed to your liking and then trim off the excess.

Following the supporting legs instructions on page 16, create two legs with three toes each. The legs should be 10cm (4in) high, with each toe approximately 5cm (2in) long. Wrap the legs and toes using grey yarn.

The feet will be slightly a different shape, depending on how you bent the wire, so to create the webbed feet, place the avocet on grey felt and draw around the feet, using the pictures for reference. Cut out the felt and glue the pieces onto the bottom of the feet, using a glue gun or craft glue. Glue the finished avocet onto a piece of driftwood, using a glue gun.

LAPWING

Lapwings are also known as "peewits", named after the sound they make. When a male lapwing is displaying to a female during the breeding season, he flies like a broken kite, flapping up into the sky and then plummeting downwards.

Materials

- 10g (⅓oz) dark green/iridescent 8-ply (DK) yarn
- 10g (⅓oz) cream 8-ply (DK) yarn
- Small amounts of 8-ply (DK) yarn in red (legs), light grey (head), black (head), and light brown (rump)
- Small amount of black felt
- Black cotton thread and sewing needle
- Two 4mm (³⁄₁₆in) black beads
- 92cm (36in) 18 gauge craft wire
- Toy stuffing

Needles

- 4mm (UK 8, US 6) knitting needles

Tension

- 6 sts and 7 rows per 2.5cm (1in)

Size

- 13cm (5in) tall including legs, 18cm (7in) long including beak

BODY (MAKE ONE)

Worked in st st. Using 4mm (UK 8, US 6) needles and brown yarn, cast on 12 sts. Work with two balls of yarn so that you do not have to carry it across the back of the cream section.

Row 1: (brown) K3, (cream) K6, (brown) K3 [12 sts].

Row 2: purl, keeping colour sequence.

Rows 3–12: repeat rows 1 and 2.

Row 13: (brown) inc 1, K2, (cream) K2, inc 2, K2, (brown) K2, inc 1 [16 sts].

Row 14: purl, keeping colour sequence.

Row 15: (brown) inc 1, K3, (cream) K3, inc 2, K3, (brown) K3, inc 1 [20 sts].

Row 16: purl, keeping colour sequence.

Row 17: (brown) inc 1, K4, (cream) K4, inc 2, K4, (brown) K4, inc 1 [24 sts].

Row 18: purl, keeping colour sequence.

Row 19: (brown) inc 1, K5, (cream) K5, inc 2, K5, (brown) K5, inc 1 [28 sts].

Row 20: purl, keeping colour sequence.

Cut off the cream yarn with which you are currently working, leaving a 15cm (6in) tail to work in at the end, and re-attach yarn to the beginning of the row. Work all in cream from this point to the end of row 26.

Lapwing's wing feather placement

Row 21: *inc 1, K5, inc 1*, rep from * to * to end [36 sts].

Rows 22–26: beginning with a purl row, work st st.

From row 27 onwards, work with two balls of cream yarn.

Row 27: (cream) K12, (black) K12, (cream) K12.

Row 28: purl, keeping colour sequence.

Row 29: (cream) K12, (black) K12, (cream) K12.

Row 30: purl, keeping colour sequence.

Row 31: (cream) K12, (black) K12, (cream) K12.

Row 32: purl, keeping colour sequence.

Row 33: (cream) K12, (black) K12, (cream) K12.

Row 34: purl, keeping colour sequence.

Row 35: (cream) K2tog, K6, K2tog, K2, (black) K12, (cream) K2, K2tog, K6, K2tog [32 sts].

Row 36: purl, keeping colour sequence.

Row 37: (cream) K2tog, K5, K2tog, K1, (black) K12, (cream) K1, K2tog, K5, K2tog [28 sts].

Row 38: purl, keeping colour sequence.

Row 39: (cream) K2tog, K4, K2tog, (black) K12, (cream) K2tog, K4, K2tog [24 sts].

Row 40: purl, keeping colour sequence.

Row 41: (cream) K2tog, K4, (black) K12, (cream) K4, K2tog [22 sts].

Row 42: purl, keeping colour sequence.

Row 43: (cream) K2tog, K3, (black) K12, (cream) K3, K2tog [20 sts].

Row 44: purl, keeping colour sequence.

Row 45: (cream) K2tog, K2, (black) K12, (cream) K2, K2tog [18 sts].

Row 46: purl, keeping colour sequence.

Cast off remaining 18 sts, keeping the colour sequence.

HEAD (MAKE ONE)

Worked in st st. Using 4mm (UK 8, US 6) needles and black yarn, cast on 20 sts. While knitting the head, work with two balls of both black and cream yarn so that you do not have to carry the yarn across the back of the work.

Row 1: knit.

Row 2: purl.

Row 3: (black) K2, (cream) K6, (grey) K4, (cream) K6, (black) K2.

Row 4: purl, keeping colour sequence.

Row 5: (black) K2, (cream) K6, (grey) K4, (cream) K6, (black) K2.

Row 6: purl, keeping colour sequence.

Row 7: (black) K2, (cream) K6, (grey) K4, (cream) K6, (black) K2.

Row 8: purl, keeping colour sequence.

Row 9: (black) K2, (cream) K6, (grey) K4, (cream) K6, (black) K2.

Work all in black until the end of the head.

Rows 10–12: beginning with a purl row, work st st.

Row 13: K2tog to end [10 sts].

Row 14: purl.

Cut yarn, thread trailing end through remaining sts on needle.

LEFT WING (MAKE ONE)

Worked in st st. Using 4mm (UK 8, US 6) needles and dark green yarn, cast on 4 sts.

Row 1: K1, inc 2, K1 [6 sts].
Row 2: purl.
Row 3: K1, inc 1, K2, inc 1, K1 [8 sts].
Row 4: purl.
Row 5: K1, inc 1, K4, inc 1, K1 [10 sts].
Row 6: purl.
Row 7: K1, inc 1, K6, inc 1, K1 [12 sts].
Row 8: purl.
Row 9: K1, inc 1, K8, inc 1, K1 [14 sts].
Row 10: purl.
Row 11: K1, inc 1, K10, inc 1, K1 [16 sts].
Row 12: purl.
Row 13: K1, K2tog, K to end [15 sts].
Row 14: purl.
Rows 15–36: repeat rows 13 and 14 eleven times more [4sts].
Row 37: K2tog to end [2 sts].
Cast off remaining sts.

RIGHT WING (MAKE ONE)

Worked in st st. Using 4mm (UK 8, US 6) needles and dark green yarn, cast on 4 sts.

Rows 1–12: work as for left wing.
Row 13: K to last 3 sts, K2tog, K1 [15 sts].
Row 14: purl.
Rows 15–36: repeat rows 13 and 14 eleven times more [4sts].
Row 37: K2tog to end [2 sts].
Cast off remaining sts.

MAKING UP

The black stitches that you cast off at the end of knitting the body piece will form the lapwing's chest. Fold the body in half and join this seam, then sew up the body and tail seam, leaving a space in the belly to stuff. Do not sew up the end of the tail. Stuff and then sew up the belly seam. Do not stuff the tail. Sew up the seam at the end of the tail, pinching it first so the tail lies flat. Sew up the head seam and stuff. Sew the head onto the body with the head seam facing the front.

Cut two wing feather pieces out of black felt, using the template. Sew one felt feather piece onto each wing using black cotton. Position each behind the knitted wing with the point extended beyond the knitted wing tip as shown. Sew each wing into position on the body – use green yarn for the knitted wing and black cotton to secure the black felt feather to the body.

To make the beak, cut out two pieces from black felt, using the template. Oversew around the edges and then sew onto the bird's face, using black cotton.

To make the crest, cut two 10cm (4in) lengths of black 8-ply (DK) yarn. Thread one onto a darning needle and take it through the top of the bird's head. Pull through until you have an equal amount of yarn on each side and then secure it in place with a knot, creating two small tufts. Repeat with the remaining piece of yarn. To finish the head, use black cotton to sew the two black beads into position as eyes.

Using 76cm (30in) of wire and following the supporting legs instructions on page 16, create legs that are 5cm (2in) high, and that have three toes, each 5cm (2in) long. Use two 8cm (3in) pieces of wire to support the legs. Wrap the legs with red 8-ply (DK) yarn.

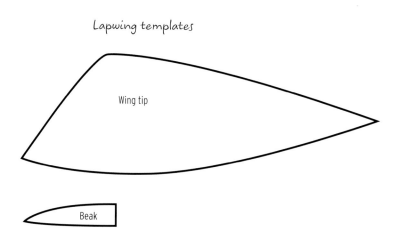

Lapwing templates

Wing tip

Beak

PUFFIN

Puffins make the most incredible noises – they sound a little like someone laughing sarcastically at a bad joke. It is a shame that they prefer to hang out on remote coastal rocky outcrops, because it would be amazing if you put fish on your garden bird table and a flock of puffins descended. Sometimes nature can be unfair.

Materials

- 15g (½oz) black 8-ply (DK) yarn
- 10g (⅓oz) cream 8-ply (DK) yarn
- Small amounts of orange 8-ply (DK) yarn
- Small amounts of grey, orange and white felt, and matching cotton threads
- Light yellow/cream embroidery thread
- Two 4mm (³⁄₁₆in) black beads
- Black cotton thread and sewing needle
- Toy stuffing

Needles

- 4mm (UK 8, US 6) knitting needles

Tension

- 6 sts and 7 rows per 2.5cm (1in)

Size

- 15cm (6in) tall, 12.5cm (5in) long including beak

NOTES

The colours in parentheses indicate the yarn you should use for the stitches that follow.

BODY (MAKE ONE)

Work with two balls of cream yarn so you do not have to carry the yarn across the back of the black section.

Worked in st st. Using 4mm (UK 8, US 6) needles and black yarn, cast on 12 sts.

Row 1: (cream) K3, (black) K6, (cream) k3.
Row 2: purl, keeping colour sequence.
Row 3: (cream) K3, (black) K6, (cream) k3.
Row 4: purl, keeping colour sequence.
Row 5: (cream) K3, (black) K6, (cream) k3.
Row 6: purl, keeping colour sequence.
Row 7: (cream) inc 1, K2, (black) K2, inc 2, K2, (cream) K2, inc 1 [16 sts].
Row 8: purl, keeping colour sequence.
Row 9: (cream) inc 1, K3, (black) K3, inc 2, K3, (cream) K3, inc 1 [20 sts].
Row 10: purl, keeping colour sequence.
Row 11: (cream) inc 1, K4, (black) K4, inc 2, K4, (cream) K4, inc 1 [24 sts].
Row 12: purl, keeping colour sequence.
Row 13: (cream) inc 1, K5, (black) K5, inc 2, K5, (cream) K5, inc 1 [28 sts].
Row 14: purl, keeping colour sequence.
Row 15: (cream) inc 1, K5, inc 1, (black) inc 1, K5, inc 2, K5, inc 1, (cream) inc 1 K5, inc 1 [36 sts].
Rows 16–22: Beginning with a purl row, work st st.
Row 23: (cream) K11, (black) K14, (cream) K11.
Row 24: purl, keeping colour sequence.
Row 25: (cream) K11, (black) K14, (cream) K11.

Row 26: purl, keeping colour sequence.

Row 27: (cream) K11, (black) K14, (cream) K11.

Row 28: purl, keeping colour sequence.

Row 29: (cream) K2tog, K10, (black) K12, (cream) K10, K2tog [34 sts].

Row 30: purl, keeping colour sequence.

Row 31: (cream) K2tog, K9, (black) K12, (cream) K9, K2tog [32 sts].

Row 32: purl, keeping colour sequence.

Row 33: (cream) K2tog, K8, (black) K12, (cream) K8, K2tog [30 sts].

Row 34: purl, keeping colour sequence.

Row 35: (cream) K2tog, K6, (black) K14, (cream) K6, K2tog [28 sts].

Row 36: purl, keeping colour sequence.

Row 37: (cream) K2tog, K4, (black) K16, (cream) K4, K2tog [26 sts].

Work all in black from this point to the end.

Row 38: purl.

Row 39: K2tog, K to last 2 sts, K2tog [24 sts].

Row 40: purl.

Row 41: *K1, K2tog*, repeat from * to * to end [16 sts].

Row 42: purl.

Row 43: K2tog to end [8 sts].

Cut yarn, thread trailing end through remaining sts on needle.

HEAD (MAKE ONE)

Worked in st st. Using 4mm (UK 8, US 6) needles and black yarn, cast on 24 sts.

Rows 1–16: beginning with a knit row, work st st.

Row 17: K2tog to end [12 sts].

Row 18: purl.

Cut yarn, thread trailing end through remaining sts on needle.

FEET (MAKE TWO)

Worked in st st. Using 4mm (UK 8, US 6) needles and orange yarn, cast on 20 sts.

Row 1: knit.

Row 2: purl.

Row 3: K2tog, K6, K2tog, K2tog, K6, K2tog [16 sts].

Row 4: purl.

Row 5: K2tog, K4, K2tog, K2tog, K4, K2tog [12 sts].

Row 6: purl.

Row 7: knit.

Row 8: purl.

Row 9: K2tog, K2, K2tog, K2tog, K2, K2tog [8 sts].

Row 10: purl.

Cast off remaining sts.

WINGS (MAKE TWO)

Worked in st st. Using 4mm (UK 8, US 6) needles and black yarn, cast on 4 sts.

Row 1: K1, inc 2, K1 [6 sts].
Row 2: purl.
Row 3: K1, inc 1, K2, inc 1, K1 [8 sts].
Row 4: purl.
Row 5: K1, inc 1, K4, inc 1, K1 [10 sts].
Row 6: purl.
Row 7: K1, inc 1, K6, inc 1, K1 [12 sts].
Row 8: purl.
Row 9: K1, inc 1, K8, inc 1, K1 [14 sts].
Rows 10–16: beginning with a purl row, work st st.
Row 17: K1, K2tog, K to last 3 sts, K2tog, K1 [12 sts].
Row 18: purl.
Row 19: K1, K2tog, K to last 3 sts, K2tog, K1 [10 sts].
Row 20: purl.
Row 21: K1, K2tog, K to last 3 sts, K2tog, K1 [8 sts].
Row 22: purl.
Row 23: K1, K2tog, K to last 3 sts, K2tog, K1 [6 sts].
Row 24: purl.
Row 25: K1, K2tog, K2tog, K1 [4 sts].
Row 26: purl.
Row 27: K2tog to end [2 sts].
Cast off remaining sts.

Puffin's feet

Puffin's beak and facial markings

Puffin templates

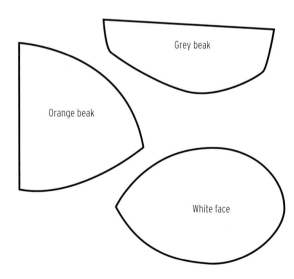

Grey beak

Orange beak

White face

MAKING UP

Sew up the body seam from top to tail, stuffing as you go. Squash the seam at the end of the tail flat and sew it up.

Pull tight the thread that you ran through the stitches at the top of the head and use it to sew up the head's side seam. Stuff the head, then run a thread around the bottom cast-on edge. Pull this thread tight to pull in the bottom of the head, and secure with a few stitches to close up the gap at the bottom. Sew the head onto the body, then sew the wings into position.

Fold each foot in half and sew up the side seam to make two triangular feet. Attach the feet to the body by sewing the cast-off edges only to the puffin's body.

Cut out two sets of templates using the respective felt colours (see templates). Sew the two white face shapes onto the head using white cotton. To make the beak, start by sewing a running stitch line of cream across the curved edge of the two grey parts of the beak. Sew the two grey parts of the beak together by overstitching the two short seams together using grey cotton. Sew the two orange pieces together, leaving open the end that attaches to the head. Slip the orange pieces inside the grey pieces. Secure the orange and grey pieces by stitching them together all round the end that will attach to the head. Stuff the beak with a little toy stuffing and sew it in place on the head using grey cotton. To finish, use black cotton to sew the two black beads onto the face for eyes.

COLLARED DOVE

Native to Europe and Asia, and recently introduced to North America, I sometimes find it hard to believe that collared doves have only been established in the UK, where I live, since the 1950s, as they are now so numerous. They can be a bit of a pest, especially if a group of them arrive and clear your bird table. People do seem to tolerate them more than other pigeons though because they look so cute.

Materials

- 15g (½oz) light grey 8-ply (DK) yarn
- Small amounts of 8-ply (DK) yarn in black and cream (markings)
- Two 3mm (⅛in) black beads
- Small amount of black felt
- Black sewing cotton and sewing needle
- 50cm (19¾in) 28 gauge copper wire
- Dusky pink embroidery thread to wrap feet
- Toy stuffing

Needles

- 4mm (UK 8, US 6) knitting needles

Tension

- 6 sts and 7 rows per 2.5cm (1in)

Size

- 18cm (7in) from top of head to tip of tail

NOTES

The colours in parentheses indicate the yarn you should use for the stitches that follow.

The pattern contains notes on working with two balls of yarn for certain sections. Doing so makes your working easier because you do not have to carry the yarn across the back of the section.

HEAD AND BODY

Worked in st st. Using 4mm (UK 8, US 6) needles and light grey yarn, cast on 12 sts.
Rows 1–18: beginning with a knit row, work st st.
Row 19: *inc 1, K4, inc 1*, rep from * to * to end [16 sts].
Row 20: purl.
Row 21: *inc 1, K6, inc 1*, rep from * to * to end [20 sts].
Row 22: purl.
Row 23: *inc 1, K8, inc 1*, rep from * to * to end [24 sts].
Row 24: purl.
Row 25: *inc 1, K10, inc 1*, rep from * to * to end [28 sts].
Row 26: purl.
Row 27: *inc 1, K12, inc 1*, rep from * to * to end [32 sts].
Row 28: purl.
Row 29: *inc 1, K14, inc 1*, rep from * to * to end [36 sts].
Rows 30–38: beginning with a purl row, work st st.
Row 39: K1, K2tog, K to last 3 sts, K2tog, K1 [34 sts].
Row 40: purl.
Row 41: K1, K2tog, K to last 3 sts, K2tog, K1 [32 sts].
Row 42: purl.
Row 43: *K2tog, K12, K2tog*, rep from * to * to end [28 sts].
Row 44: purl.

Row 45: *K2tog, K10, K2tog*, rep from * to * to end [24 sts].
Row 46: purl.
Row 47: *K2tog, K8, K2tog*, rep from * to * to end [20 sts].
Row 48: purl.
Row 49: K1, K2tog, K to last 3 sts, K2tog, K1 [18 sts].
Rows 50–58: beginning with a purl row, work st st.
Row 59: K2tog to end [9 sts].
Row 60: purl.
Row 61: K1, *K2tog*, rep from * to * to end [5 sts].
Cut yarn, thread trailing end through remaining sts on needle.

WINGS (MAKE TWO)

Worked in st st. Using 4mm (UK 8, US 6) needles and light grey yarn, cast on 4 sts.
Row 1: K1, inc 2, K1 [6 sts].
Row 2: purl.
Row 3: K1, inc 1, K2, inc 1, K1 [8 sts].
Row 4: purl.
Row 5: K1, inc 1, K4, inc 1, K1 [10 sts].
Row 6: purl.
Row 7: K1, inc 1, K6, inc 1, K1 [12 sts].
Row 8: purl.
Row 9: K1, inc 1, K8, inc 1, K1 [14 sts].
Row 10: purl.
Row 11: K1, inc 1, K10, inc 1, K1 [16 sts].
Rows 12–16: beginning with a purl row, work st st.
Row 17: K1, K2tog, K to last 3 sts, K2tog, K1 [14 sts].
Row 18: purl.
Row 19: K1, K2tog, K to last 3 sts, K2tog, K1 [12 sts].
Row 20: purl.

From row 21 onwards, work with two balls of black yarn.

Row 21: (black) K1, K2tog, K1, (grey) K4, (black) K1, K2tog, K1 [10 sts].

Row 22: purl, keeping colour sequence.

Row 23: (black) K1, K2tog, K1, (grey) K2, (black) K1, K2tog, K1 [8 sts].

Work all in black from this point to the end of the wing.

Row 24: purl.

Row 25: K1, K2tog, K to last 3 sts, K2tog, K1 [6 sts].

Row 26: purl.

Row 27: K1, K2tog, K2tog, K1 [4 sts].

Row 28: purl.

Row 29: K2tog to end [2 sts].

Row 30: purl.

Cast off remaining 2 sts.

MAKING UP

Sew up the body seam from head to tail, leaving a gap for stuffing in the belly. Do not sew up the seam at the end of the tail, where you cast on. Stuff the body, but leave the tail unstuffed. Sew up the belly gap. Sew up the seam at the end of the tail, pinching it first so the tail lies flat.

Sew the wings into position using the darning needle and light grey yarn. Cut out a black felt beak, using the template, and sew into position using black cotton. Sew the two beads onto the head for eyes. Using black and cream 8-ply (DK) yarn, sew black and white stripes on the back of the bird's neck.

Follow the posable legs instructions on page 15 to create legs using 50cm (19¾in) of copper wire, wrapped with pink cotton.

Collared dove beak template

MAGPIE

'One for sorrow, two for joy...' It is probably best to knit a pair of these clever corvids, then. In folklore, magpies have a reputation for collecting shiny objects and stealing jewellery. You can knit a nest (see page 126) for your thieving magpie to give him somewhere to stash his treasures.

Materials

- 30g (1oz) black 8-ply (DK) yarn
- 10g (⅓oz) navy blue 8-ply (DK) yarn
- 10g (⅓oz) cream 8-ply (DK) yarn
- Small amount of black felt
- Black cotton thread and sewing needle
- Two 5mm (½in) black beads
- One chenille stem and sticky tape
- 60cm (23½in) 28 gauge copper wire
- Toy stuffing

Needles

- 4mm (UK 8, US 6) knitting needles

Tension

- 6 sts and 7 rows per 2.5cm (1in)

Size

- 28cm (11in) from top of head to tip of tail

NOTES

The colours in parentheses indicate the yarn you should use for the stitches that follow. The pattern contains notes on working with two balls of yarn for certain sections. Doing so makes your working easier because you do not have to carry the yarn across the back of the section.

BODY AND HEAD (MAKE ONE)

Worked in st st. Using 4mm (UK 8, US 6) needles and navy blue yarn, cast on 10 sts.

Rows 1–30: beginning with a knit row, work st st.

Row 31: K1, inc 1, K6, inc 1, K1 [12 sts].

Row 32: purl.

Change to black yarn.

Row 33: *inc 1, K4, inc 1*, rep from * to * to end [16 sts].

Row 34: purl.

Row 35: *inc 1, K6, inc 1*, rep from * to * to end [20 sts].

Row 36: purl.

Row 37: *inc 1, K8, inc 1*, rep from * to * to end [24 sts].

Row 38: purl.

Row 39: *inc 1, K10, inc 1*, rep from * to * to end [28 sts].

Row 40: purl.

Row 41: *inc 1, K12, inc 1*, rep from * to * to end [32 sts].

From row 42 onwards, work with two balls of cream yarn.

Row 42: (cream) P11, (black) P10, (cream) P11.

Row 43: (cream) K1, inc 1, K9, (black) K10, (cream) K9, inc 1, K1 [34 sts].

Row 44: purl, keeping colour sequence.

Row 45: (cream) K1, inc 1, K10, (black) K10, (cream) K10, inc 1, K1 [36 sts].

Rows 46–60: beginning with a purl row, work st st, keeping the colour sequence.

Work all in black from this point to the end.

Row 61: K1, K2tog, K to last 3 sts, K2tog, K1 [34 sts].

Row 62: purl.

Row 63: K1, K2tog, K to last 3 sts, K2tog, K1 [32 sts].

Row 64: purl.

Row 65: K1, K2tog, K to last 3 sts, K2tog, K1 [30 sts].

Row 66: purl.

Row 67: K1, K2tog, K to last 3 sts, K2tog, K1 [28 sts].

Row 68: purl.

Row 69: K1, K2tog, K to last 3 sts, K2tog, K1 [26 sts].

Row 70: purl.

Row 71: K1, K2tog, K to last 3 sts, K2tog, K1 [24 sts].

Row 72: purl.

Row 73: K1, K2tog, K to last 3 sts, K2tog, K1 [22 sts].

Rows 74–80: beginning with a purl row, work st st.

Row 81: K2tog to end [11 sts].

Row 82: purl.

Row 83:, K1, *K2tog*, rep from * to * to end [6 sts].

Row 84: purl.

Cut yarn, thread trailing end through remaining sts on needle.

RIGHT WING (MAKE ONE)

Worked in st st. Using 4mm (UK 8, US 6) needles and black yarn, cast on 4 sts.

Row 1: K1, inc 2, K1 [6 sts].
Row 2: purl.
Row 3: K1, inc 1, K2, inc 1, K1 [8 sts].
Row 4: purl.
Row 5: (black) K1, inc 1, K3, (blue) K1, inc 1, K1 [10 sts].
Row 6: purl, keeping colour sequence.
Row 7: (black) K1, inc 1, K3, (blue) K3, inc 1, K1 [12 sts].
Row 8: purl, keeping colour sequence.
Row 9: (black) K1, inc 1, K4, (blue) K4, inc 1, K1 [14 sts].
Row 10: purl, keeping colour sequence.
Row 11: (black) K1, inc 1, K4, (blue) K6, inc 1, K1 [16 sts].
Row 12: purl, keeping colour sequence.
Row 13: (black) K5, (blue) K11.
Row 14: purl, keeping colour sequence.
Row 15: (black) K4, (blue) K12.
Row 16: purl, keeping colour sequence.
Row 17: (black) K2, (blue) K14.
Work all in blue from this point to the end of the wing.
Rows 18–20: beginning with a purl row, work st st.
Row 21: K1, K2tog, K to last 3 sts, K2tog, K1 [14 sts].
Row 22: purl.
Row 23: K1, K2tog, K to last 3 sts, K2tog, K1 [12 sts].
Row 24: purl.
Row 25: K1, K2tog, K to last 3 sts, K2tog, K1 [10 sts].
Row 26: purl.
Row 27: K1, K2tog, K to last 3 sts, K2tog, K1 [8 sts].
Row 28: purl.
Row 29: knit.
Row 30: purl.
Row 31: K1, K2tog, K to last 3 sts, K2tog, K1 [6 sts].
Row 32: purl.
Row 33: K1, K2tog, K2tog, K1 [4 sts].
Row 34: purl.
Row 35: knit.
Row 36: purl.
Row 37: K2tog to end [2 sts].
Cast off remaining sts.

LEFT WING (MAKE ONE)

Worked in st st. Using 4mm (UK 8, US 6) needles and black, yarn cast on 4 sts.

Row 1: K1, inc 2, K1 [6 sts].
Row 2: purl.
Row 3: K1, inc 1, K2, inc 1, K1 [8 sts].
Row 4: purl.
Row 5: (blue) K1, inc 1, K1, (black) K3, inc 1, K1 [10 sts].
Row 6: purl, keeping colour sequence.
Row 7: (blue) K1, inc 1, K3, (black) K3, inc 1, K1 [12 sts].
Row 8: purl, keeping colour sequence.
Row 9: (blue) K1, inc 1, K4, (black) K4, inc 1, K1 [14 sts].
Row 10: purl, keeping colour sequence.
Row 11: (blue) K1, inc 1, K6, (black) K4, inc 1, K1 [16 sts].
Row 12: purl, keeping colour sequence.
Row 13: (blue) K11, (black) K5 [16 sts].
Row 14: purl, keeping colour sequence.
Row 15: (blue) K12, (black) K4 [16 sts].
Row 16: purl, keeping colour sequence.
Row 17: (blue) K14, (black) K2 [16 sts].
Work all in blue from this point to the end of the wing.
Rows 18–37: work as for the right wing.
Cast off remaining sts.

WING FLASHES (MAKE TWO)

Worked in st st. Using 4mm (UK 8, US 6) needles and cream yarn, cast on 5 sts. Work in st st until your piece measures 7cm (2¾in) from the cast-on edge, finishing with a purl row. Cast off.

Magpie's wing flash

Magpie beak template

MAKING UP

Sew up the head and body seam, stuffing as you go. Stop before you get to the tail. Follow the instructions on page 14 to create a supported tail using the chenille stem. Do not stuff the tail. Sew up the seam at the end of the tail, pinching it first so that the tail lies flat.

Sew the cream flashes onto the wings, positioning them so that they cover the area where the black stitching changes to blue (use the pictures for reference). Sew the wings onto the body.

Cut out two beak shapes from black felt, using the template. Sew the two pieces together using black cotton and leave open the end that will be attached to the head. Gently stuff with a little polyester stuffing and sew to the head, using black cotton. Sew the two beads into position for eyes.

Follow the posable legs instruction on page 15 to create legs using 60cm (23½in) of black copper wire, wrapped with black 8-ply (DK) yarn.

OYSTERCATCHER

Oystercatchers are one of my favourite birds. You can spot them pottering around at low tide on beaches and estuaries, using their long beaks to look for lunch in the sand. They are easy to recognise because they have bright red eyes, and look like they are wearing an old-fashioned dinner jacket.

Materials
- 10g (⅓oz) black 8-ply (DK) yarn
- 20g (¾oz) cream 8-ply (DK) yarn
- 20g (¾oz) red 8-ply (DK) yarn
- Two 4mm (³⁄₁₆oz) red beads
- Red felt and matching cotton thread
- Sewing needle
- 79cm (31in) 18 gauge wire
- Toy stuffing

Needles
- 4mm (UK 8, US 6) knitting needles

Tension
- 6 sts and 7 rows per 2.5cm (1in)

Size
- 13cm (5in) tall, 15cm (6in) long

NOTES
The colours in parentheses indicate the yarn you should use for the stitches that follow.

BODY AND HEAD (MAKE ONE)
Worked in st st. Using 4mm (UK 8, US 6) needles and cream yarn, cast on 12 sts. Work with two balls of cream yarn so you do not have to carry the yarn across the back of the black section.

Row 1: (cream) K3, (black) K6, (cream) K3.
Row 2: purl, keeping colour sequence.
Row 3: (cream) K3, (black) K6, (cream) K3.
Row 4: purl, keeping colour sequence.
Row 5: (cream) K3, (black) K6, (cream) K3.
Row 6: purl, keeping colour sequence.
Row 7: (cream) inc 1, K2, (black) K2, inc 2, K2, (cream) K2, inc 1 [16 sts].
Row 8: purl, keeping colour sequence.
Row 9: (cream) inc 1, K3, (black) K3, inc 2, K3, (cream) K3, inc 1 [20 sts].
Row 10: purl, keeping colour sequence.
Row 11: (cream) inc 1, K4, (black) K4, inc 2, K4, (cream) K4, inc 1 [24 sts].
Row 12: purl, keeping colour sequence.
Row 13: (cream) inc 1, K6, (black) K4, inc 2, K4, (cream) K6, inc 1 [28 sts].
Row 14: purl, keeping colour sequence.
Row 15: (cream) inc 1, K5, inc 2, (black) K5, inc 2, K5, (cream) inc 2, K5, inc 1 [36 sts].
Rows 16–28: beginning with a purl row, work st st, keeping colour sequence.
Row 29: (cream) K2tog, K5, K2tog, K2tog, (black) K5, K2tog, K2tog, K5, (cream) K2tog, K2tog, K5, K2tog [28 sts].
Rows 30–32: beginning with a purl row, work st st, keeping colour sequence.
Row 33: (cream) K2tog, K3, K2tog, K2tog, (black) K3, K2tog, K2tog, K3, (cream) K2tog, K2tog, K3, K2tog [20 sts].

Rows 34–36: beginning with a purl row, work st st, keeping colour sequence.

Work all in black from this point to the end.

Row 37: K8, K2tog, K2tog, K8 [18 sts].

Row 38: purl.

Row 39: K7, K2tog, K2tog, K7 [16 sts].

Rows 40–44: beginning with a purl row, work st st.

Row 45: *K1, K2tog, K1*, rep from * to * to end [12 sts].

Row 46: purl.

Row 47: K2tog to end [6 sts].

Row 48: purl.

Run yarn through remaining sts on needle.

LEFT WING (MAKE ONE)

Worked in st st. Using 4mm (UK 8, US 6) needles and cream yarn, cast on 4 sts.

Row 1: inc 1, K2, inc 1 [6 sts].

Row 2: purl.

Row 3: inc 1, K4, inc 1 [8 sts].

Row 4: purl.

Change to black yarn.

Row 5: inc 1, K6, inc 1 [10 sts].

Row 6: purl.

Row 7: inc 1, K8, inc 1 [12 sts].

Row 8: purl.

Row 9: (cream) K3, (black) K9.

Row 10: purl, keeping colour sequence.

Row 11: (cream) K3, (black) K9.

Row 12: purl, keeping colour sequence.

Row 13: (cream) K3, (black) K9.

Row 14: purl, keeping colour sequence.

Row 15: (cream) K3, (black) K9.

Row 16: purl, keeping colour sequence.

Row 17: (cream) K1, K2tog, (black) K9 [11 sts].

Row 18: purl, keeping colour sequence.

Row 19: (cream) K2tog, (black) K9 [10 sts].

Work all in black yarn from this point to the end.

Row 20: purl.

Row 21: K2tog, K6, K2tog [8 sts].

Rows 22–24: beginning with a purl row, work st st.

Row 25: K2tog, K4, K2tog [6 sts].

Row 26: purl.

Row 27: K2tog, K2, K2tog [4 sts].

Row 28: purl.

Row 29: K2tog to end [2 sts].

Cast off remaining sts on needle.

RIGHT WING (MAKE ONE)

Worked in st st. Using 4mm (UK 8, US 6) needles and cream yarn, cast on 4 sts.

Rows 1–8: work as for the left wing.

Row 9: (black) K9, (cream) K3.

Row 10: purl, keeping colour sequence.

Row 11: (black) K9, (cream) K3.

Row 12: purl, keeping colour sequence.

Row 13: (black) K9, (cream) K3.

Row 14: purl, keeping colour sequence.

Row 15: (black) K9, (cream) K3.

Row 16: purl, keeping colour sequence.

Row 17: (black) K9, (cream) K2tog, K1 [11 sts].

Row 18: purl, keeping colour sequence.

Row 19: (black) K9, (cream) K2tog [10 sts].

Work all in black yarn from this point to the end.

Row 20: purl.

Row 21: K2tog, K6, K2tog [8 sts].

Rows 22–24: beginning with a purl row, work st st.

Row 25: K2tog, K4, K2tog [6 sts].

Row 26: purl.

Row 27: K2tog, K2, K2tog [4 sts].

Row 28: purl.

Row 29: K2tog to end [2 sts].

Cast off remaining sts on needle.

MAKING UP

Sew up the body seam from the top of the head to the tail, leaving a space for stuffing. Do not sew up the flat end of the tail, where you cast on. Stuff the body with toy stuffing and sew up the rest of the head-to-tail seam. Next, squash the flat end of the tail so that the top of the tail is made up of black stitches and the bottom of the tail is white stitches (see picture above right), then sew up the tail seam. Sew the wings onto the body, positioning the white flashes at the bottom.

To make the beak, cut out a beak shape from red felt using the template. Fold in half lengthways and sew the side seam, keeping open the end of the beak that will attach to the head. Cut a 10cm (4in) piece of wire and fold over the top half inch to make a blunt end. Insert the blunt end into the beak. You may not be able to get it all the way down to the beak tip – just gently insert it as far as it will go. Position the beak on the head, inserting the pointed end of the wire into the head for support. Sew the beak into position using red cotton, then sew two red beads onto the head for eyes.

To make the tail, sew loops of black yarn along the flat tail seam, making each loop 2–2.5cm (½–1in) in length. Leave a little variation in size to avoid it looking too neat and contrived.

Follow the supporting legs instructions on page 16 to create legs, wrapping 69cm (27in) of wire with red 8-ply (DK) yarn. Bend the wire to make the legs approximately 6.5cm (2½in) high, with three toes measuring 3.5cm (1½in) long on each leg.

Detail of the underside of the oystercatcher's tail, showing the belly seam

Oystercatcher's head and beak

Oystercatcher beak template

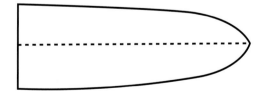

OSPREY

This is is not just any old osprey; this is Monty, the male osprey from the Dyfi Osprey Project in Wales. Monty has unusual orange eyes (adult osprey's eyes are usually yellow) and a penchant for mullet. Monty usually returns to Wales from his migration in April, and you can watch him and his family on the Dyfi Osprey Project webcams. It is more addictive than any soap opera, so be warned. If you would like to knit an adult osprey that is not Monty, just change the eyes from orange to yellow. Don't worry; it will still enjoy the fish.

Materials

- ↓ 50g (1¾oz) cream 8-ply (DK) yarn
- ↙ 20g (¾oz) dark brown 8-ply (DK) yarn
- ↓ Small amounts of light brown and black 8-ply (DK) yarn
- ↙ Orange or yellow felt for eyes
- ↙ Two 4mm (³⁄₁₆in) black beads
- ↓ Black cotton
- ↓ Black felt
- ↓ 90cm (35½in) of 18 gauge copper wire
- ↙ Toy stuffing

Needles

- ↙ 4mm (UK 8, US 6) knitting needles

Tension

- ↓ 6 sts and 7 rows per 2.5cm (1in)

Size

- ↙ 25.5cm (10in) from head to tail, 8cm (3¼in) wide

OSPREY

> ### NOTES
> The colours in parentheses indicate the yarn you should use for the stitches that follow.
>
> The pattern contains notes on working with two balls of yarn for certain sections. Doing so makes your working easier because you do not have to carry the yarn across the back of the section.

BODY (MAKE ONE)

Worked in st st. Using 4mm (UK 8, US 6) needles and dark brown cast on 20 sts.

Row 1: knit.

Row 2: purl.

From this point onwards, work with two balls of cream yarn.

Row 3: (cream) K5, (brown) K10, (cream) K5.

Row 4: purl, keeping colour sequence.

Row 5: (dark brown) knit.

Row 6: (dark brown) purl.

Row 7: (cream) K5, (brown) K10, (cream) K5.

Row 8: purl, keeping colour sequence.

Row 9: (dark brown) knit.

Row 10: (dark brown) purl.

Row 11: (cream) K5, (brown) K10, (cream) K5.

Row 12: purl, keeping colour sequence.

Row 13: (dark brown) knit.

Row 14: (dark brown) purl.

Row 15: (cream) inc 1, K3, (dark brown) K5, inc 2, K5, (cream) K3, inc 1 (24 sts].

Row 16: purl, keeping colour sequence.

Row 17: (cream) inc 1, K5, (dark brown) K5, inc 2, K5, (cream) K5, inc 1 [28 sts].

Row 18: purl, keeping colour sequence.

Row 19: (cream) inc 1, K7, (dark brown) K5, inc 2, K5, (cream) K7, inc 1 [32 sts].

Row 20: purl, keeping colour sequence.

Row 21: (cream) inc 1, K9, (dark brown) K5, inc 2, K5, (cream) K9, inc 1 [36 sts].

Rows 22–47: beginning with a purl row, work st st, keeping colour sequence.

Row 48: (cream) K2tog, K10, (dark brown) K12, (cream) K10, K2tog [34 sts].
Row 49: purl, keeping colour sequence.
Row 50: (cream) K2tog, K10, (dark brown) K10, (cream) K10, K2tog [32 sts].
Row 51: purl, keeping colour sequence.
Row 52: (cream) K2tog, K10, (dark brown) K8, (cream) K10, K2tog [30 sts].
Row 53: purl, keeping colour sequence.
Work all in cream from this point to the end of the body.
Row 54: K2tog, K to last 2 sts, K2tog [28 sts].
Row 55: purl.
Row 56: K2tog, K to last 2 sts, K2tog [26 sts].
Row 57: purl.
Row 58: K2tog to end [13 sts].
Row 59: purl.
Cut yarn, thread trailing end through remaining sts on needle.

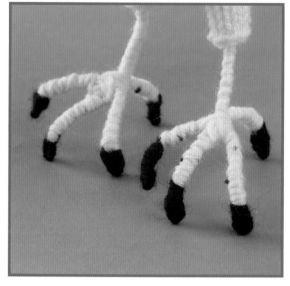

Osprey's talons

HEAD (MAKE ONE)

Worked in st st. Using 4mm (UK 8, US 6) needles and cream yarn cast on 22 sts. Work with two balls of brown from row 1 onwards.
Row 1: (dark brown) K3, (cream) K16, (dark brown) K3.
Row 2: (dark brown) P3, (cream) P16, (dark brown) P3.
Row 3: (dark brown) K3, (cream) K16, (dark brown) K3.
Row 4: (dark brown) P3, (cream) P16, (dark brown) P3.
Row 5: (dark brown) K4, (cream) K14, (dark brown) K4.
Row 6: (dark brown) P5, (cream) P12, (dark brown) P5.
Row 7: (dark brown) K8, (cream) K6, (dark brown) K8.
From this point onwards, work with two balls of cream yarn.
Row 8: (cream) P2, (dark brown) P18, (cream) P2.
Row 9: (cream) K3, (dark brown) K16, (cream) K3.
Row 10: (cream) P4, (dark brown) P14, (cream) P4.
Row 11: (cream) K8, (dark brown) K6, (cream) K8.
Work all in cream from this point to the end of the body.
Row 12: purl.
Row 13: knit.
Row 14: purl.
Row 15: K2tog to end [11 sts].
Row 16: purl.
Cut yarn, thread trailing end through remaining sts on needle.

Monty's orange eye flash

WINGS (MAKE TWO)

Worked in st st. Using 4mm (UK 8, US 6) needles and dark brown yarn, cast on 4 sts.

Row 1: K1, inc 2, K1 [6 sts].

Row 2: purl.

Row 3: K1, inc 1, K2, inc 1, K1 [8 sts].

Row 4: purl.

Row 5: K1, inc 1, K4, inc 1, K1 [10 sts].

Row 6: purl.

Row 7: K1, inc 1, K6, inc 1, K1 [12 sts].

Row 8: purl.

Row 9: K1, inc 1, K8, inc 1, K1 [14 sts].

Rows 10–36: beginning with a purl row, work st st.

Row 37: K1, K2tog, K to last 3 sts, K2tog, K1 [12 sts].

Row 38: purl.

Row 39: K1, K2tog, K to last 3 sts, K2tog, K1 [10 sts].

Row 40: purl.

Row 41: K1, K2tog, K to last 3 sts, K2tog, K1 [8 sts].

Row 42: purl.

Row 43: K1, K2tog, K to last 3 sts, K2tog, K1 [6 sts].

Row 44: purl.

Row 45: K1, K2tog, K2tog, K1 [4 sts].

Row 46: purl.

Row 47: K2tog to end [2 sts].

Cast off remaining sts.

LEG TOPS (MAKE TWO)

Worked in st st. Using 4mm (UK 8, US 6) needles and cream yarn cast on 8 sts.

Rows 1–6: beginning with a knit row, work st st.

Cast off remaining sts.

Detail of the underside of the osprey's tail, showing the distinctive striped pattern

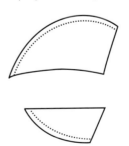

Osprey beak template

MAKING UP

Sew up the body seam from the top to the tail, stuffing as you go. Do not stuff the tail. Flatten the tail so that the tail end seam lies flat, and then sew up. Sew up the head seam from top to bottom, stuff, and then sew into position on the body with the seam facing the back. Pin the wings into position on the body. There will be a little white gap between the top of the wing and the dark brown stripes on the head. Embroider four or five large running stitches using dark brown yarn over this white gap to soften the transition between the stripe and the white body. Sew the wings into position.

Cut out two orange or yellow felt circles with a diameter of 1cm (⅜in), for eyes. Position a black bead in the middle of each circle and sew the felt and beads onto the head using black cotton (you do not need to sew around the edge of the eye, sewing the bead onto the head will keep the felt in position).

To make the beak, using the templates, cut out two upper beak pieces, and two lower beak pieces, all from black felt. Sew the two upper pieces together along the dotted line. Sew the two lower pieces together along the dotted line. Insert the lower beak inside the upper beak, using the pictures as reference. Secure the two pieces together with a few stitches along the seam where the two pieces meet. Stuff with a tiny amount of stuffing and sew onto the head using black cotton.

Follow the posable legs instructions on page 15 to create legs using 90cm (35½in) of 18 gauge copper wire. The legs should be approximately 6cm (2½in) long, each with four toes, approximately 4cm (1½in) in length. Bend over the tip of each toe to make claws. Wrap the legs and toes in cream 8-ply (DK) yarn. Do not wrap the claws. Wrap the claws in black 8-ply (DK) yarn. Secure the black yarn by running it though the underneath of the cream yarn wrapped toes. Once you have wrapped the claws, wrap the legs again with another layer of cream (use this layer to hide any black yarn ends).

When you have wrapped the legs with yarn, take the knitted leg tops and sew these into position at the top of each leg. Wrap each leg top tightly around each wire leg and sew into position.

Sew a scattering of light brown Swiss darning stitches (see page 17) on the bird's belly. Sew a few dark brown Swiss darning stitches on the top and front of the bird's head.

MONTY'S MULLET

Materials

- Small amounts of light grey and dark grey 8-ply (DK) yarn
- Two 4mm (³⁄₁₆in) black beads
- Black cotton
- White felt
- Toy stuffing

Needles

- 4mm (UK 8, US 6) knitting needles

Tension

- 6 sts and 7 rows per 2.5cm (1in)

Size

- 15cm (6in) long

MULLET BODY (MAKE ONE)

Worked in st st. Using 4mm (UK 8, US 6) needles and light grey yarn, cast on 10 sts.

Row 1: knit.
Row 2: purl.
Row 3: *K1, inc 1, K1, inc 1, K1*, rep from * to * to end [14 sts].
Row 4: purl.
Row 5: *K1, inc 1, K3, inc 1, K1*, rep from * to * to end [18 sts].
Row 6: purl.
Row 7: *K1, inc 1, K5, inc 1, K1*, rep from * to * to end [22 sts].
Rows 8–30: beginning with a purl row, work st st.
Row 31: *K1, K2tog, K5, K2tog, K1*, rep from * to * to end [18 sts].
Row 32: purl.
Row 33: knit.
Row 34: purl.
Row 35: *K1, K2tog, K3, K2tog, K1*, rep from * to * to end [14 sts].
Row 36: purl.
Row 37: K2tog to end [7 sts].
Row 38: purl.
Run yarn through remaining sts on needle.

MULLET TAIL (MAKE ONE)

Worked in garter st. Using 4mm (UK 8, US 6) needles and dark grey yarn, cast on 4 sts.

Row 1: K1, inc 2, K1 [6 sts].

Row 2: knit.

Row 3: K1, inc 1, K2, inc 1, K1 [8 sts].

Row 4: knit.

Row 5: K1, inc 1, K4, inc 1, K1 [10 sts].

Row 6: knit.

Row 7: K1, inc 1, K6, inc 1, K1 [12 sts].

Row 8: K6, turn and work rows 9–12 only on the six stitches you have just knitted.

Row 9: K1, K2 tog, K2tog, K1 [4 sts].

Row 10: knit.

Row 11: K2tog to end [2 sts].

Row 12: K2tog [1 st].

Run yarn through remaining st. Cut yarn and re-attach to remaining six stitches on needle. Work rows 8–12 on these six remaining sts. Run yarn through remaining st.

MULLET FINS (MAKE TWO)

Worked in garter st. Using 4mm (UK 8, US 6) needles and dark grey yarn, cast on 6 sts.

Row 1: knit.

Row 2: knit.

Row 3: K1, K2tog, K2tog, K1 [4 sts].

Row 4: knit.

Row 5: K2tog to end [2 sts].

Row 6: knit.

Row 7: K2tog [1 st].

Run yarn though remaining st on needle.

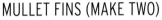

MAKING UP

Sew up the seam from the top of the head to the end of the body, stuffing as you go. The finished fish should be fairly flat, so do not overstuff. Do not sew up the tail seam (where you cast on at the beginning). Insert the end of the dark grey tail into the hole at the end of the body and sew up the seam to attach the tail to the body. Sew the fins into position on either side of the body.

Cut out two 1cm (⅜in) circles out of white felt for eyes. Position a black bead in the middle of each circle and sew the felt and beads onto the head using black cotton. You do not need to sew around the edge of the eye, sewing the bead onto the head will keep the felt in position.

KINGFISHERS

There is something magical about a kingfisher. You can be walking along by a river and then there's a sudden flash of vibrant orange and blue as a kingfisher dives into the river after a meal.

Having identical plumage, the way to tell a male and a female kingfisher apart is by their beaks – the male's beak is all black, but the female has orange on the bottom part of her beak. Just remember that the female wears lipstick!

Materials
- Small amounts of 8-ply (DK) yarn in blue, orange and cream
- Black felt
- Black cotton
- Two 5mm (¼in) black beads
- 60cm (23½in) 28 gauge copper wire
- Red yarn or embroidery thread to wrap feet
- Toy stuffing

For female only:
- Orange felt
- Orange cotton in the same shade as the felt

Needles
- 4mm (UK 8, US 6) knitting needles

Tension
- 6 sts and 7 rows per 2.5cm (1in)

Size
- 10cm (4in) tall

NOTES
The colours in parentheses indicate the yarn you should use for the stitches that follow.

The pattern contains notes on working with two balls of yarn for certain sections. Doing so makes your working easier because you do not have to carry the yarn across the back of the section.

BODY AND HEAD (MAKE ONE)
Worked in st st. Using 4mm (UK 8, US 6) needles and blue yarn, cast on 12 sts.
Work with two balls of orange yarn.
Row 1: (orange) K3, (blue) K6, (orange) K3.
Row 2: purl, keeping colour sequence.
Row 3: (orange) K3, (blue) K6, (orange) K3.
Row 4: purl, keeping colour sequence.
Row 5: (orange) inc 1, K2, (blue) K2, inc 2, K2, (orange) K2, inc 1 [16 sts].
Row 6: purl, keeping colour sequence.
Row 7: (orange) inc 1, K3, (blue) K3, inc 2, K3, (orange) K3, inc 1 [20 sts].
Row 8: purl, keeping colour sequence.
Row 9: (orange) inc 1, K4, (blue) K4, inc 2, K4, (orange) K4, inc 1 [24 sts].
Row 10: purl, keeping colour sequence.
Row 11: (orange) inc 1, K5, (blue) K5, inc 2, K5, (orange) K5, inc 1 [28 sts].
Rows 12–16: starting with a purl row, work st st, keeping colour sequence.
Row 17: (orange) K2tog, K6, (blue) K12, (orange) K6, K2tog [26 sts].
Row 18: (orange) P8, (blue) P10, (orange) P8.
Row 19: (orange) K2tog, K7, (blue) K8, (orange) K7, K2tog [24 sts].
Row 20: purl, keeping colour sequence.

Kingfisher's wing

Female kingfisher's facial markings and beak

Work with two balls of cream yarn from this row onwards.

Row 21: (cream) K3, (blue) K2, (cream) K4, (blue) K6, (cream) K4, (blue) K2, (cream) K3.

Row 22: purl, keeping colour sequence.

Row 23: (cream) K3, (blue) K2, (orange) K4, (blue) K6, (orange) K4, (blue) K2, (cream) K3.

Row 24: purl, keeping colour sequence.

Row 25: (cream) K2, (blue) K2, (orange) K4, (blue) K8, (orange) K4, (blue) K2, (cream) K2.

Work all in blue from this point to the end.

Row 26: purl.

Row 27: K2tog to end [12 sts].

Row 28: purl.

Row 29: K2tog to end [6 sts].

Cut yarn, thread trailing end through remaining sts on needle.

WING (MAKE TWO)

Worked in st st. Using 4mm (UK 8, US 6) needles and blue yarn, cast on 4 sts.

Row 1: K1, inc 2, K1 [6 sts].

Row 2: purl.

Row 3: K1, inc 1, K to last 2 sts, inc 1, K1 [8 sts].

Row 4: purl.

Row 5: K1, inc 1, K to last 2 sts, inc 1, K1 [10 sts].

Rows 6–10: beginning with a purl row, work st st.

Row 11: K1, K2tog, K4, K2tog, K1 [8 sts].

Row 12: purl.

Row 13: K1, K2tog, K2, K2tog, K1 [6 sts].

Row 14: purl.

Row 15: K1, K2tog, K2tog, K1 [4 sts].

Row 16: purl.

Row 17: K2tog to end [2 sts].

Cast off remaining sts.

MAKING UP

Sew the seam from the top of the head to the end of the tail, stuffing as you go. Sew up the seam at the end of the tail, where you cast on, pinching it first so that the tail lies flat. Sew the wings into position.

For the male's beak, cut out two identical pieces from black felt, using the template. Sew the two pieces together around the edges, leaving the end that will attach to the beak open. Stuff with a little polyester stuffing as you go (it will be hard to stuff at the end as the opening is small). Sew the beak into position on the head, using black cotton.

For the female's beak, cut out one beak piece in black felt, and one in orange felt. Sew together around the edges using orange cotton and then stuff and sew into position as for the male, with the orange part of the beak positioned to the bottom. (The orange stitching will be visible on the black part of the beak. If this bothers you as much as it bothered me, then simply dab the visible stitching with a black permanent marker pen – make sure that you use one hundred per cent cotton thread if you want to do this.)

Using black cotton, sew two black beads onto the head as eyes. Follow the posable legs instruction on page 15 to create feet using 60cm (23¼in) of copper wire, wrapped with red yarn.

Kingfisher beak template

HOOPOE

When I was a child, I always wanted to see a hoopoe. It was the most exotic looking bird in my parents' rather stuffy book of British birds. In my head, a hoopoe was about the size of an osprey and had magical powers, like a phoenix. It was not until doing research for this book that I realised it was as small as a thrush. Despite the diminutive size, it is still an incredibly beautiful bird. Sadly, I still haven't seen a real one – so a knitted hoopoe will need to do for now.

NOTES
The colours in parentheses indicate the yarn you should use for the stitches that follow.

The pattern contains notes on working with two balls of yarn for certain sections. Doing so makes your working easier because you do not have to carry the yarn across the back of the section.

Materials
- 20g (¾oz) peach 8-ply (DK) yarn
- Small amounts of 8-ply (DK) yarn in black, cream and grey
- One black and two white chenille stems, and sticky tape
- 84cm (33in) length of 18 gauge wire
- Black felt
- Black cotton thread and sewing needle
- Two 5mm (¼in) black beads
- Toy stuffing

Needles
- 4mm (UK 8, US 6) knitting needles

Tension
- 6 sts and 7 rows per 2.5cm (1in)

Size
- 18cm (7in) tall excluding the crest

BODY AND HEAD (MAKE ONE)
Worked in st st. Using 4mm (UK 8, US 6) needles and black yarn, cast on 12 sts.

Rows 1–16: beginning with a knit row, work st st.
From row 17 onwards, work with two balls of cream yarn.
Row 17: (cream) inc 1, K2, (peach) K2, inc 2, K2, (cream) K2, inc 1 [16 sts].
Row 18: purl, keeping colour sequence.
Row 19: (cream) inc 1, K3, (peach) K3, inc 2, K3, (cream) K3, inc 1 [20 sts].
Row 20: purl, keeping colour sequence.
Row 21: (cream) inc 1, K4, (peach) K4, inc 2, K4, (cream) K4, inc 1 [24 sts].
Row 22: purl, keeping colour sequence.
Row 23: (cream) inc 1, K5, (peach) K5, inc 2, K5, (cream) K5, inc 1 [28 sts].
Row 24: purl, keeping colour sequence.
Row 25: (cream) inc 1, K6, (peach) K6, inc 2, K6, (cream) K6, inc 1 [32 sts].
Row 26: purl, keeping colour colour sequence.
Row 27: (cream) K7, (peach) K18, (cream) K7.
Row 28: (cream) P6, (peach) P20, (cream) P6.
Row 29: (cream) K5, (peach) K22, (cream) K5.
Row 30: (cream) P4, (peach) P24, (cream) P4.
Row 31: (cream) K3, (peach) K26, (cream) K3.
Work all in peach from this point to the end.
Rows 32–36: beginning with a purl row, work st st.
Row 37: K1, K2tog, K to last 3 sts, K2tog, K1 [30 sts].
Row 38: purl.
Row 39: K1, K2tog, K to last 3 sts, K2tog, K1 [28 sts].
Row 40: purl.
Row 41: K1, K2tog, K to last 3 sts, K2tog, K1 [26 sts].
Row 42: purl.
Row 43: K1, K2tog, K to last 3 sts, K2tog, K1 [24 sts].
Row 44: purl.
Row 45: K1, K2tog, K to last 3 sts, K2tog, K1 [22 sts].
Row 46: purl.
Row 47: K1, K2tog, K to last 3 sts, K2tog, K1 [20 sts].
Rows 48–58: beginning with a purl row, work st st.
Row 59: K2tog to end (10 sts).
Row 60: purl.
Row 61: K2tog to end (5 sts).
Cut yarn, thread trailing end through remaining sts on needle.

WING (MAKE TWO)

Worked in st st. Using 4mm (UK 8, US 6) needles and peach yarn, cast on 4 sts.

Row 1: K1, inc 2, K1 [6 sts].
Row 2: purl.
Row 3: K1, inc 1, K to last 2 sts, inc 1, K1 [8 sts].
Row 4: purl.
Row 5: K1, inc 1, K to last 2 sts, inc 1, K1 [10 sts].
Row 6: purl.
Row 7: K1, inc 1, K to last 2 sts, inc 1, K1 [12 sts].
Row 8: (black) purl.
Row 9: (black) knit.
Row 10: (black) purl.
Row 11: (black) knit.
Row 12: (cream) purl.
Row 13: (cream) knit.
Row 14: (cream) purl.
Row 15: (cream) knit.
Row 16: (black) purl.
Row 17: (black) knit.
Row 18: (black) purl.
Row 19: (black) knit.
Row 20: (cream) purl.
Row 21: (cream) K1, K2tog, K to last 3 sts, K2tog, K1 [10 sts].
Row 22: (cream) purl.
Row 23: (cream) K1, K2tog, K to last 3 sts, K2tog, K1 [8 sts].
Row 24: (black) purl.
Row 25: (black) K1, K2tog, K to last 3 sts, K2tog, K1 [6 sts].
Row 26: (black) purl.
Row 27: (black) K1, K2tog, K2tog, K1 [4 sts].
Row 28: (black) purl.
Row 29: (black) K2tog to end [2 sts].
Row 30: (black) purl.
Cast off remaining sts.

Hoopoe beak template

MAKING UP

Sew the front seam from the top of head to an inch away from the base of the tail, stuffing as you go. Take a black chenille stem, bend over the top 1cm (⅜in) and secure with sticky tape. Insert into tail with the sticky tape end at the end of the tail and the sharp end pointing into the stuffing of the belly. Sew up the tail seam around the chenille stem and sew up the remainder of the belly seam. Next, sew the wings into position.

To make the beak, cut out two pieces from the templates using black felt, and oversew together all round the edges using black cotton – leave the end that attaches to the head open.

Cut a 7.5cm (3in) length of wire and bend it into the curved shape of the beak. Gently insert it into the beak. Note that it does not have to go all the way to the end. There will be approximately 2.5cm (1in) of wire sticking out of the base of the beak – poke the protruding wire into the bird's head and sew the beak into position using black cotton.

To make the hoopoe's crest, take a 7.5cm (3in) length of white chenille stem. Bend over the top 1cm (⅜in) and then wrap with peach yarn, using the same technique as creating a toe in the posable legs instructions on page 15. Leave 1cm (⅜in) at the bottom of the chenille stem unwrapped so that you can poke it into the head when you have finished. Do not worry if little tufts of white chenille stem show through, as the hoopoe has a scattering of white plumage in the crest, alongside the peach.

Using black 8-ply (DK) yarn, embroider black stripes on the crest feathers as shown in the pictures. Push the unwrapped 1cm (⅜in) of the chenille stem into the hoopoe's head and secure using a few peach 8-ply (DK) yarn stitches. Repeat the process until you have made three feathers. Sew on two black beads for eyes, using black cotton.

Follow the posable legs instruction on page 15 to create the legs, using a 76cm (30in) piece of stiff craft wire and wrapping it in grey 8-ply (DK) yarn. Bend the wire so that each toe is approximately 2.5cm (1in) long, and each leg is 2.5cm (1in) tall.

Hoopoe's wing markings

PHEASANT

Male pheasants always make me think of autumn. Maybe it is their brown mottled plumage that echoes the colours of the season. This fine knitted specimen would look very much at home perched on top of a fence post or log.

Materials

- 15g (½oz) dark brown tweed effect aran yarn (rump and wing speckles)
- 10g (⅓oz) golden brown tweed effect 8-ply (DK) yarn
- 20g (¾oz) oatmeal brown aran yarn (back and tail)
- 20g (¾oz) dark brown 8-ply (DK) yarn (chest)
- Small amounts of 8-ply (DK) yarn in cream (neck ring), dark green (head), and black (tail stripes)
- Red felt and matching cotton thread
- Oatmeal felt and matching cotton thread
- Two 4mm (⅛in) yellow beads and matching cotton thread
- Sewing needle
- Five or six glass pebbles
- Toy stuffing

Needles

- 4mm (UK 8, US 6) knitting needles

Tension

- 6 sts and 7 rows per 2.5cm (1in)

Size

- 31cm (12in) long excluding beak

NOTES

The colours in parentheses indicate the yarn you should use for the stitches that follow.

The pattern contains notes on working with two balls of yarn for certain sections. Doing so makes your working easier because you do not have to carry the yarn across the back of the section.

BODY (MAKE ONE)

Worked in st st. Using 4mm (UK 8, US 6) needles, cast on 8 sts. Work with two balls of dark brown tweed yarn.

Row 1: (dark brown tweed) inc 2, (oatmeal) inc 4, (dark brown tweed) inc 2 [16 sts].

Row 2: purl, keeping colour sequence.

Row 3: knit, keeping colour sequence.

Row 4: purl, keeping colour sequence.

Row 5: (dark brown tweed) inc 6, (oatmeal) inc 4, (dark brown tweed) inc 6 [32 sts].

Row 6: purl, keeping colour sequence.

Row 7: knit, keeping colour sequence.

Row 8: purl, keeping colour sequence.

Row 9: (dark brown tweed) inc 1, K3, inc 1, K3, inc 1, K3 (oatmeal) inc 1, K3, inc 1, K3, (dark brown tweed) inc 1, K3, inc 1, K3, inc 1, K3 [40 sts].

Row 10: purl, keeping colour sequence.

Row 11: knit, keeping colour sequence.

Row 12: purl, keeping colour sequence.

From row 13 onwards, work with two balls of golden tweed yarn.

Row 13: (dark brown tweed) K15, (golden brown tweed) K2, (oatmeal) K6, (golden brown tweed) K2, (dark brown tweed) K15.

Row 14: purl, keeping colour sequence.

Row 15: (dark brown tweed) K15, (golden brown tweed) K3, (oatmeal) K4, (golden brown tweed) K3, (dark brown tweed) K15.

Row 16: purl, keeping colour sequence.

Row 17: (dark brown tweed) K15, (golden brown tweed) K4, (oatmeal) K2, (golden brown tweed) K4, (dark brown tweed) K15.

Row 18: purl, keeping colour sequence.

Row 19: (dark brown tweed) K15, (golden brown tweed) K10, (dark brown tweed) K15.

Row 20: purl, keeping colour sequence.

From row 21 onwards, work with two balls of dark brown 8-ply (DK) yarn.

Row 21: (dark brown) K15, (golden brown tweed) K10, (dark brown) K15.

Row 22: purl, keeping colour sequence.

Row 23: (dark brown) K15, (golden brown tweed) K10, (dark brown) K15.

Row 24: purl, keeping colour sequence.

Row 25: (dark brown) K15, (golden brown tweed) K10, (dark brown) K15.

Row 26: purl, keeping colour sequence.

Row 27: (dark brown) K15, (golden brown tweed) K10, (dark brown) K15.

Row 28: purl, keeping colour sequence.

Row 29: (dark brown) K1, K2tog, K13, (golden brown tweed) K8, (dark brown) K13, K2tog, K1 [38 sts].

Row 30: (dark brown) P16, (golden brown tweed) P6, (dark brown) P16.

Work in dark brown 8-ply (DK) only from this point to the end of the body.

Row 31: K1, K2tog, K to last 3 sts, K2tog, K1 [36 sts].

Row 32: purl.

Row 33: K1, K2tog, K to last 3 sts, K2tog, K1 [34 sts].

Row 34: purl.

Row 35: K1, K2tog, K to last 3 sts, K2tog, K1 [32 sts].

Row 36: purl.

Row 37: K1, K2tog, K to last 3 sts, K2tog, K1 [30 sts].

Cast off remaining 30 sts.

HEAD (MAKE ONE)

Worked in st st. Using 4mm (UK 8, US 6) needles and dark brown 8-ply (DK) yarn, cast on 20 sts.

Row 1: (dark brown) knit.

Row 2: (dark brown) purl.

Row 3: (cream) knit.

Row 4: (cream) purl.

Rows 5–12: (dark green) beginning with a knit row, work st st.

Row 13: (dark green) K2tog to end (10 sts).

Row 14: (dark green) purl.

Row 15: (dark green) K2tog to end (5 sts).

Row 16: (dark green) purl.

Cut yarn, thread trailing end through remaining sts on needle.

WINGS (MAKE TWO)

Worked in st st. Using 4mm (UK 8, US 6) needles and golden brown tweed yarn, cast on 4 sts.

Row 1: K1, inc 2, K1 [6 sts].

Row 2: purl.

Row 3: K1, inc 1, K2, inc 1, K1 [8 sts].

Row 4: purl.

Row 5: K1, inc 1, K4, inc 1, K1 [10 sts].

Row 6: purl.

Row 7: K1, inc 1, K6, inc 1, K1 [12 sts].

Row 8: purl.

Row 9: K1, inc 1, K8, inc1, K1 [14 sts].

Rows 10–14: beginning with a purl row, work st st.

Row 15: K1, K2tog, K8, K2tog, K1 [12 sts].

Pheasant's facial markings

Row 16: purl.
Row 17: K1, K2tog, K6, K2tog, K1 [10 sts].
Rows 18–20: beginning with a purl row, work st st.
Row 21: K1, K2tog, K4, K2tog, K1 [8 sts].
Rows 22–24: beginning with a purl row, work st st.
Row 25: K1, K2tog, K2, K2tog, K1 [6 sts].
Row 26: purl.
Row 27: K1, K2tog, K2tog, K1 [4 sts].
Row 28: purl.
Row 29: K2tog to end [2 sts].
Row 30: purl.
Cast off remaining sts.

LONG TAIL FEATHER (MAKE ONE)
Worked in st st. Using 4mm (UK 8, US 6) needles and oatmeal yarn, cast on 10 sts.
Rows 1–4: (oatmeal) beginning with a knit row, work st st.
Rows 5–6: (black) beginning with a knit row, work st st.
Rows 7–10: (oatmeal) beginning with a knit row, work st st.
Rows 11–12: (black) beginning with a knit row, work st st.
Rows 13–16: (oatmeal) beginning with a knit row, work st st.
Rows 17–18: (black) beginning with a knit row, work st st.
Rows 19–22: (oatmeal) beginning with a knit row, work st st.
Rows 23–24: (black) beginning with a knit row, work st st.
Rows 25–28: (oatmeal) and beginning with a knit row, work st st.

Row 29–30: (black) beginning with a knit row, work st st.
Rows 31–34: (oatmeal) beginning with a knit row, work st st.
Rows 35–36: (black) beginning with a knit row, work st st.
Work all in oatmeal from this point to the end of the tail feather.
Rows 37–38: beginning with a knit row, work st st.
Row 39: K2tog to end (5 sts).
Row 40: purl.
Row 41: K1, K2tog, K2tog (3 sts).
Row 42: purl.
Run yarn through remaining sts on needle.

SHORT TAIL FEATHER (MAKE ONE)
Worked in st st. Using 4mm (UK 8, US 6) needles and oatmeal yarn, cast on 8 sts.
Rows 1–24: work as for the long tail feather [8 sts].
Work all in oatmeal from this point to the end of the short tail feather.
Row 25: knit.
Row 26: purl.
Row 27: K2tog to end [4 sts].
Row 28: purl.
Row 29: K2tog to end [2 sts].
Row 30: purl.
Cut yarn, thread trailing end through remaining sts on needle.

Detail of the stripes on the pheasant's tail feathers

MAKING UP

Fold the body in half and sew up the front seam from top to bottom. Next sew up the belly seam, stuffing as you go and inserting the glass pebbles into the base of the bird to help it stand up properly. Sew up the side seam of the head, stuff, and sew into position on the body, using dark brown yarn and with the seam facing the back.

Sew up the seams of the tail feathers and sew into position on the bird's bottom, with the longer feather on top of the shorter one.Before sewing the wings into position, embroider a scattering of speckles using Swiss darning stitches (see page 17) onto each wing, using dark brown tweed effect yarn. Sew into position using light brown tweed effect yarn.

Cut out two face shapes from red felt, using the template, and sew into position on the head, using red cotton. Cut out the two beak pieces from oatmeal felt, using the templates, and sew together using oatmeal cotton, leaving open the end that will be attached to the head. Gently stuff with a little polyester stuffing. Sew onto the head using oatmeal cotton. Use yellow cotton to sew two yellow beads onto the head for eyes.

Pheasant templates

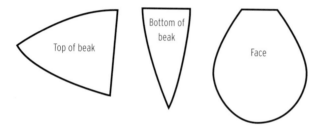

Top of beak

Bottom of beak

Face

Pheasant's underside

SNOWY OWLS

Snowy owls nest in the Arctic tundra. Luckily this knitting pattern gives you the opportunity to get close to a snowy owl without leaving the comfort of your own home.

This pattern allows you to knit a snowy owl with wings at rest or one with the wings outstretched - these wings are supported by chenille sticks and knitted in sections.

Materials

↯ 40g (1½oz) of cream 8-ply (DK) yarn
↯ 40g (1½oz) of black 2-ply (lace) yarn
↯ White chenille stems
↯ Small amounts of black and yellow felt and matching cotton thread
↯ Sewing needle
↯ Eight or nine glass pebbles
↯ Toy stuffing

Needles

↯ 4mm (UK 8, US 6) knitting needles

Tension

↯ 6 sts and 7 rows per 2.5cm (1in)

Size

↯ 15cm (6in) tall, 23cm (9in) wide from wingtip to wingtip

NOTES

The snowy owl can be made up with its wings outstretched or folded in. Whichever you choose, you will need one body and head and one set of wings. The materials listed above are sufficient to make either version.

SNOWY OWL BODY AND HEAD (MAKE ONE)

Worked in st st. Using 4mm (UK 8, US 6) needles and cream yarn, cast on 16 sts.

Row 1: *inc 1, K6, inc 1*, repeat from * to * to end [20 sts].
Row 2: purl.
Row 3: *inc 1, K3, inc 1*, repeat from * to * to end [28 sts].
Row 4: purl.
Row 5: *inc 1, K5, inc 1*, repeat from * to * to end [36 sts].
Row 6: purl.
Row 7: *inc 1, K7, inc 1*, repeat from * to * to end [44 sts].
Row 8: purl.
Row 9: *inc 1, K20, inc 1*, repeat from * to * to end [48 sts].
Rows 10–28: beginning with a purl row, work st st.
Row 29: *K2tog, K20, K2tog*, repeat from * to * to end [44 sts].
Row 30: purl.
Row 31: *K2tog, K18, K2tog*, repeat from * to * to end [40 sts].
Row 32: purl.
Row 33: *K2tog, K16, K2tog*, repeat from * to * to end [36 sts].
Row 34: purl.
Row 35: *K2tog, K14, K2tog*, repeat from * to * to end [32 sts].
Rows 36–48: beginning with a purl row, work st st.
Row 49: K2tog to end [16 sts].
Row 50: purl.
Row 51: K2tog to end [8 sts].
Cut yarn, thread trailing end through remaining sts on needle.

OUTSTRETCHED WINGS

TOP WING FEATHER (MAKE TWO)
Worked in st st. Using 4mm (UK 8, US 6) needles and cream yarn, cast on 10 sts.

Rows 1–12: beginning with a knit row, work st st.

Row 13: K2tog, K6, K2tog [8 sts].

Rows 14–22: beginning with a purl row, work st st.

Row 23: K2tog, K4, K2tog [6 sts].

Rows 24–26: beginning with a purl row, work st st.

Row 27: K2tog, K2, K2tog [4 sts].

Row 28: purl.

Cast off remaining sts.

MIDDLE WING FEATHER (MAKE TWO)
Worked in st st. Using 4mm (UK 8, US 6) needles and cream yarn, cast on 8 sts.

Rows 1–8: beginning with a knit row, work st st.

Row 9: K2tog, K4, K2tog [6 sts].

Rows 10–18: beginning with a purl row, work st st.

Row 19: K2tog, K2, K2tog [4 sts].

Rows 20–24: beginning with a purl row, work st st.

Cast off remaining sts.

BOTTOM WING FEATHER (MAKE TWO)
Worked in st st. Using 4mm (UK 8, US 6) needles and cream yarn, cast on 20 sts.

Row 1–6: beginning with a knit row, work st st.

Row 7: K8, K2tog, K2tog, K8 [18 sts].

Rows 8–12: beginning with a purl row, work st st.

Row 13: K7, K2tog, K2tog, K7 [16 sts].

Rows 14–16: beginning with a purl row, work st st.

Row 17: *K1, K2tog, K1*, repeat from * to * to end [12 sts].

Row 18: purl.

Row 17: *K1, K2tog, K1*, repeat from * to * to end [9 sts].

Row 18: purl.

Row 19: K1, *K2tog*, repeat from * to * to end [5 sts].

Row 20: purl.

Cast off remaining sts.

FOLDED WINGS

WINGS (MAKE TWO)

Worked in st st. Using 4mm (UK 8, US 6) needles and cream yarn, cast on 4 sts.

Row 1: K1, inc 2, K1 [6 sts].
Row 2: purl.
Row 3: K1, inc 1, K2, inc 1, K1 [8 sts].
Row 4: purl.
Row 5: K1, inc 1, K4, inc 1, K1 [10 sts].
Row 6: purl.
Row 7: K1, inc 1, K6, inc 1, K1 [12 sts].
Row 8: purl.
Row 9: K1, inc 1, K8, inc 1, K1 [14 sts].
Row 10: purl.
Row 11: knit.
Row 12: purl.
Row 13: K1, K2tog, K8, K2tog, K1 [12 sts].
Row 14: purl.
Row 15: K1, K2tog, K6, K2tog, K1 [10 sts].
Row 16: purl.
Row 17: K1, K2tog, K4, K2tog, K1 [8 sts].
Row 18: purl.
Row 19: K1, K2tog, K2, K2tog, K1 [6 sts].
Row 20: purl.
Row 21: K1, K2tog, K2tog, K1 [4 sts].
Row 22: purl.
Row 23: K2tog to end [2 sts].
Row 24: purl.
Cast off remaining sts.

Snowy owl templates

MAKING UP WITH UPRIGHT WINGS

Sew up the side seam, starting at the head. Start stuffing when you have sewn up approximately three quarters of the side seam, then insert the glass pebbles to weigh the base of the owl down and help give it stability. Tuck stuffing all around the pebbles so they do not poke through the knitted fabric surface. Sew up the remaining side seam and, when the bird is stuffed to your liking, sew up the bottom seam.

To make the wings, start by assembling the feathers. Each wing is made up of three feathers. The top two feathers have chenille stems inside them to support the wings.

To assemble the top wing feather, take a 12.75cm (5in) length of chenille stem and lay it down the length of the feather. Sew up the side seam, enclosing the chenille stem in the feather. You will not be able to get the chenille stem all the way down to the tip of the feather as it will be too narrow – just get it down as far as possible. You will end up with approximately 2.5cm (1in) sticking out of the end of the feather. This will later be attached to the body. Repeat this process to assemble the middle wing feather. To assemble the bottom wing feather, fold it in half along the cast-on stitches. Sew up the seam along the long side of the triangle that you have formed.

Sew the top wing feather into position at the side of the owl's body to make the top of the wing. Poke the chenille stem into the body and sew the feather to the body. Repeat this process with the middle wing feather, positioning it just under the top wing feather. Sew the bottom wing feather into position under the middle wing feather, with the side seam facing the top so that it is against the middle wing feather.

With the back of the wing facing you, oversew the bottom wing feather to the middle wing feather, sewing for approximately 2.5cm (1in) from the body. Repeat the process, sewing the top wing feather to the middle wing feather.

Using the templates, cut out two eye shapes from yellow felt, and two pupils from black felt. Sew the pupils onto the eyes, using black thread (or use white glue). Cut out a beak shape from black felt, using the template. Sew the beak and eyes onto the owl's face (or attach using white glue).

Use 2-ply (lace) black yarn and a sharp darning needle to embroider black feather details on the owl in Swiss darning stitch (see page 17): a ring of stitching around the neck, leaving a space at the front; a cluster of stitches on the top of the head; a scattering of stitches on the belly.

MAKING UP WITH FOLDED WINGS

Make up and stuff the body, as for the snowy owl with raised wings. Sew the two wings into position on the side of the bird's body. Make the facial features and embroider the black feather details as for the snowy owl with outstretched wings.

If you would like to make your owl wink, substitute one of the yellow eyes for a small crescent of black felt.

WOODPECKER

Here's the opportunity to welcome a woodpecker in your home without having to put up with endless holes appearing in all of your wooden furniture.

Materials
- 10g (⅓oz) green 8-ply (DK) yarn
- 10g (⅓oz) cream 8-ply (DK) yarn
- Small amounts of 8-ply (DK) yarn in charcoal grey (for tail), lighter grey (for feet), yellow-grey, red-grey and black
- Small amounts of black and white felt
- Black cotton
- Chenille stem
- Two 4mm (⅛in) black beads
- 76cm (30in) piece of 20 gauge craft wire
- Toy stuffing

Needles
- 4mm (UK 8, US 6) knitting needles

Tension
- 6 sts and 7 rows per 2.5cm (1in)

Size
- 20cm (8in) from top of head to tip of tail

NOTES
The colours in parentheses indicate the yarn you should use for the stitches that follow.

The pattern contains notes on working with two balls of yarn for certain sections. Doing so makes your working easier because you do not have to carry the yarn across the back of the section.

BODY AND HEAD (MAKE ONE)
Worked in st st. Using 4mm (UK 8, US 6) needles and charcoal yarn, cast on 24 sts.

Row 1: knit.
Row 2: purl.
Row 3: K4, K2tog, K2tog, K8, K2tog, K2tog, K4 [20 sts].
Row 4: purl.
Row 5: (green) K3, K2tog, K2tog, K6, K2tog, K2tog, K3 [16 sts].
Row 6: (green) purl.
Row 7: (grey) K2, K2tog, K2tog, K4, K2tog, K2tog, K2 [12 sts].
Row 8: (grey) purl.
Row 9: (green) knit.
Row 10: (green) purl.
Row 11: (grey) knit.
Row 12: (grey) purl.
From this point on, work with two balls of green and charcoal yarn.
Row 13: (green) K5, (yellow) K2, (green) K5.
Row 14: (green) P4, (yellow) P4, (green) P4.
Row 15: (green) K3, (yellow) K6, (green) K3.
Row 16: (green) P2, (yellow) P8, (green) P2.
From this point on, work with two balls of cream yarn.
Row 17: (cream) K2, (yellow) K8, (cream) K2.
Row 18: (cream) P2, (yellow) P8, (cream) P2.
Row 19: (cream) inc 1, K2, (yellow) K2, inc 2, K2, (cream) K2, inc 1 [16 sts].

Row 20: purl, keeping colour sequence.

Row 21: (cream) inc 1, K3, (yellow) K3, inc 2, K3, (cream) K3, inc 1 [20 sts].

Row 22: purl, keeping colour sequence.

Row 23: (cream) inc 1, K4, (yellow) K4, inc 2, K4, (cream) K4, inc 1 [24 sts].

Row 24: purl, keeping colour sequence.

Row 25: (cream) inc 1, K5, (yellow) K5, inc 2, K5, (cream) K5, inc 1 [28 sts].

Row 26: purl, keeping colour sequence.

Row 27: (cream) inc 1, K8, (yellow) K4, inc 2, K4, (cream) K8, inc 1 [32 sts].

Row 28: purl, keeping colour sequence.

Row 29: (cream) K10, (green) K12, (cream) K10.

Row 30: purl, keeping colour sequence.

Row 31: (cream) K10, (green) K12, (cream) K10.

Row 32: purl, keeping colour sequence.

Row 33: (cream) K10, (green) K12, (cream) K10.

Row 34: purl, keeping colour sequence.

Row 35: (cream) K10, (green) K12, (cream) K10.

Row 36: purl.

Row 37: (cream) K10, (green), K12, (cream) K10.

Row 38: purl.

Row 39: (cream) K1, K2tog, K8, (green) K10, (cream) K8, K2tog, K1 [30 sts].

Row 40: (cream) P11, (green) P8, (cream) P11.

Row 41: (cream) K1, K2tog, K8, (green) K8, (cream) K8, K2tog, K1 [28 sts].

Row 42: purl, keeping colour sequence.

Row 43: (cream) K1, K2tog, K7, (green) K8, (cream) K7, K2tog, K1 [26 sts].

Row 44: purl, keeping colour sequence.

Row 45: (cream) K1, K2tog, K6, (green) K8, (cream) K6, K2tog, K1 [24 sts].

Row 46: purl, keeping colour sequence.

Row 47: (cream) K1, K2tog, K6, (green) K6, (cream) K6, K2tog, K1 [22 sts].

Row 48: purl, keeping colour sequence.

Row 49: (cream) K1, K2tog, K5, (green) K6, (cream) K5, K2tog, K1 [20 sts].

Row 50: (cream) P7, (red) P6, (cream) P7.

Row 51: (cream) K7, (red) K6, (cream) K7.

Row 52: (cream) P7, (red) P6, (cream) P7.

From this point on, work with two balls of black yarn.

Row 53: (black) K2, (cream) K5, (red) K6, (cream) K5, (black) K2.

Row 54: (black) P3, (cream) P4, (red) P6, (cream) P4, (black) P3.

Row 55: (black) K4, (cream) K3, (red) K6, (cream) K3, (black) K4.

Row 56: (black) P4, (cream) P3, (red) P6, (cream) P3, (black) P4.

Row 57: (black) K4, (cream) K3, (red) K6, (cream) K3, (black) K4.

Row 58: (black) P4, (cream) P3, (red) P6, (cream) P3, (black) P4.

Row 59: (black) K4, (cream) K3, (red) K6, (cream) K3, (black) K4.

Work all in red from this point to the end.

Row 60: purl.

Row 61: K2tog to end [10 sts].

Row 62: purl.

Row 63: K2tog to end [5 sts].

Cut yarn, thread trailing end through remaining sts on needle.

WINGS (MAKE TWO)

Worked in st st. Using 4mm (UK 8, US 6) needles and green yarn, cast on 4 sts.

Row 1: K1, inc 2, K1 [6 sts].
Row 2: purl.
Row 3: K1, inc 1, K to last 2 sts, inc 1, K1 [8 sts].
Row 4: purl.
Row 5: K1, inc 1, K to last 2 sts, inc 1, K1 [10 sts].
Row 6: purl.
Row 7: K1, inc 1, K to last 2 sts, inc 1, K1 [12 sts].
Rows 8–20: beginning with a purl row, work st st.
Row 21: K1, K2tog, K to last 3 sts, K2tog, K1 [10 sts].
Row 22: purl.
Row 23: K1, K2tog, K to last 3 sts, K2tog, K1 [8 sts].
Row 24: purl.
Row 25: K1, K2tog, K to last 3 sts, K2tog, K1 [6 sts].
Row 26: purl.
Row 27: K1, K2tog, K2tog, K1 [4 sts].
Row 28: purl.
Row 29: K2tog to end [2 sts].
Row 30: purl.
Cast off remaining sts.

MAKING UP

Sew up the body seam from the top of the head to the end of the tail, stuffing as you go. Do not stuff the tail, and do not sew up the seam at the bottom of the tail where you cast on. Squash the tail flat so that it lies horizontal, and then sew up this seam to give the tail the correct shaping. Sew the wings into position.

To create the beak, cut out two identical pieces of black felt using the template. Sew around the edges of the beak, leaving the end that attaches to the head open. Cut a 6.5cm (2½in) piece of chenille stem and insert it into the beak. There should be approximately 1.25cm (½in) sticking out of the beak. Position the beak onto the head, and poke the 1.25cm (½in) of chenille stem into the head stuffing. Sew the beak onto the head using black cotton.

Cut out two circles of white felt which are slightly larger than the black beads. Position the felt circles on the black part of the face where you want the eyes to sit. Secure each piece of felt into position with a small stitch in the middle (you can use black cotton for this as it will not be visible), then sew a black bead into the middle of each white circle using black cotton.

Follow the posable legs instruction on page 15 to make legs using a 76cm (30in) piece of wire to create four toes on each foot, each approximately 2.5cm (1in) in length. Wrap the legs and feet using grey 8-ply (DK) yarn.

Woodpecker's back and tail markings

Woodpecker beak template

ROBIN

Robins have been known to fight to the death over territorial disputes. which is why you only ever see them in ones and twos. Bear this in mind if you are planning to knit more than a pair. or you may end up with polyester stuffing all over the room.

Materials
- 10g (⅓oz) light brown 8-ply (DK) yarn
- Small amounts of cream 8-ply (DK) yarn
- 50cm (19¾in) 28 gauge black copper wire
- Black crochet cotton thread to wrap feet
- Two 3mm (⅛in) black beads
- Black cotton thread and sewing needle
- Small amounts of black and red felt, and matching cotton thread
- Toy stuffing

Needles
- 4mm (UK 8, US 6) knitting needles

Tension
- 6 sts and 7 rows per 2.5cm (1in)

Size
- 10cm (4in) from top of head to tip of tail

NOTES
The colours in parentheses indicate the yarn you should use for the stitches that follow.

The pattern contains notes on working with two balls of yarn for certain sections. Doing so makes your working easier because you do not have to carry the yarn across the back of the section.

BODY AND HEAD (MAKE ONE)
Worked in st st. Start knitting at the tail end. Using 4mm (UK 8, US 6) needles and light brown yarn, cast on 6 sts.

Rows 1–10: beginning with a knit row, work st st.

Row 11: inc 1, K to last st, inc 1 [8 sts].

Row 12: purl.

From row 13 onwards, work with two balls of cream yarn.

Row 13: (cream) inc 1, (brown) K2, inc 2, K2, (cream) inc 1 [12 sts].

Row 14: purl, keeping colour sequence.

Row 15: (cream) inc 1, K1, (brown) K3, inc 2, K3, (cream) K1, inc 1 [16 sts].

Row 16: purl, keeping colour sequence.

Row 17: (cream) inc 1, K2, (brown) K4, inc 2, K4, (cream) K2, inc 1 [20 sts].

Row 18: purl, keeping colour sequence.

Row 19: (cream) inc 1, K3, (brown) K5, inc 2, K5, (cream) K3, inc 1 [24 sts].

Row 20: purl, keeping colour sequence.

Row 21: (cream) K2tog, K3, (brown) K14, (cream) K3, K2tog [22 sts].

Row 22: purl, keeping colour sequence.

Row 23: (cream) K2tog, K2, (brown) K14, (cream) K2, K2tog [20 sts].

Row 24: purl, keeping colour sequence.

Work all in brown from this point to the end.

Row 25: K2tog, K16, K2tog [18 sts].

Row 26: purl.

Row 27: K2tog, K14, K2tog [16 sts].

Row 28: purl.

Row 29: K2tog to end [8 sts].

Row 30: purl.

Cut yarn, thread trailing end through remaining sts on needle.

WINGS (MAKE TWO)

Using 4mm (UK 8, US 6) needles and light brown yarn, cast on 4 sts.

Row 1: K1, inc 2, K1 [6 sts].

Row 2: purl.

Row 3: K1, inc 1, K2, inc 1, K1 [8 sts].

Rows 4–8: beginning with a purl row, work st st.

Row 9: K1, K2tog, K2, K2tog, K1 [6 sts].

Row 10: purl.

Row 11: K1, K2tog, K2tog, K1 [4 sts].

Row 12: purl.

Row 13: K2tog to end [2 sts].

Cast off remaining sts.

MAKING UP

Pull the thread tight through the stitches at the top of the head and use this thread to sew up the front seam, changing to cream to sew up the breast seam. Leave a space at the bottom for stuffing. Stuff, then sew up the remainder of the seam. Sew up the tail seam and the tip of the tail. Do not stuff the tail.

Cut out a breast from red felt using the template and sew it into position using red thread. The tip of the felt shape should be aligned with where you have pulled the thread tight at the top of the head.

Using the template, cut out a beak from black felt. Fold in half and sew up the seam using black thread, then sew into position. Sew on two black beads for eyes. Sew the wings into position.

Follow the posable legs instruction on page 15 to create legs using 50cm (19¾in) of black copper wire, wrapped with black crochet cotton.

Robin templates

Breast

Beak

SPARROW

These little brown birds often get overlooked in the garden in favour of more colourful avian visitors but they are a pleasure to watch. Sparrows are very sociable and are often seen hopping around in a large group enjoying each other's company (unlike starlings, who hang around in a large group and bicker like children in the back seat of a car on a long journey).

Materials
- 7g (¼oz) light oatmeal 8-ply (DK) yarn (tail and belly)
- 3g (⅛oz) dark brown 8-ply (DK) yarn (wings)
- Small amounts of 8-ply (DK) yarn in grey (top of head), light brown (back of head), and black (face)
- Small amount of black 2-ply (lace) yarn
- Small amount of black felt
- Black cotton thread and sewing needle
- Two 5mm (¼in) black beads
- 60cm (23½in) 28 gauge copper wire
- Pink-brown embroidery thread to wrap feet
- Toy stuffing

Needles
- 4mm (UK 8, US 6) knitting needles

Tension
- 6 sts and 7 rows per 2.5cm (1in)

Size
- 16.5cm (6½in) from top of head to tip of tail

NOTES
The colours in parentheses indicate the yarn you should use for the stitches that follow.

The pattern contains notes on working with two balls of yarn for certain sections. Doing so makes your working easier because you do not have to carry the yarn across the back of the section.

BODY AND HEAD
Worked in st st. Using 4mm (UK 8, US 6) needles and light oatmeal yarn, cast on 6 sts.

Rows 1–16: Beginning with a knit row, work st st.
Row 17: inc 1, K to last st, inc 1 [8 sts].
Row 18: purl.
Row 19: *inc 1, K2, inc 1*, rep from * to * to end [12 sts].
Row 20: purl.
Row 21: *inc 1, K4, inc 1*, rep from * to * to end [16 sts].
Row 22: purl.
Row 23: *inc 1, K6, inc 1*, rep from * to * to end [20 sts].
Row 24: purl.
Row 25: *inc 1, K8, inc 1*, rep from * to * to end [24 sts].
Row 26: purl.
Row 27: *inc 1, K10, inc 1*, rep from * to * to end [28 sts].
Rows 28–32: Beginning with a purl row, work st st.

From row 33 onwards, work with two balls of light oatmeal yarn.

Row 33: (light oatmeal) K10, (light brown) K8, (light oatmeal) K10 [28 sts].

Row 34: purl, keeping colour sequence.

Row 35: (light oatmeal) K2tog, K9, (light brown) K6, (light oatmeal) K9, K2tog [26 sts].

Row 36: purl, keeping colour sequence.

Row 37: (light oatmeal) K2tog, K8, (light brown) K6, (light oatmeal) K8, K2tog [24 sts].

Row 38: purl, keeping colour sequence.

Row 39: (light oatmeal) K2tog, K5, K2tog, (light brown) K6, (light oatmeal) K2tog, K5, K2tog [20 sts].

Row 40: purl, keeping colour sequence.

Row 41: K2tog, K to the last 2 sts, keeping the the colour sequence, K2tog (18 sts).

Rows 42–44: Beginning with a purl row, work st st, keeping the colour sequence.

From row 45 onwards, work with two balls of black yarn.

Row 45: (black) K4, (light brown) K10, (black) K4.

Row 46: (black) P4, (light brown) P10, (black) P4.

Row 47: (black) K4, (light brown) K10, (black) K4.

Change to grey and work in this colour to the end of the head.

Row 48: purl.

Row 49: K2tog to end [9 sts].

Row 50: purl.

Cut yarn, thread trailing end through remaining sts on needle.

WINGS (MAKE TWO)

Worked in st st. Using 4mm (UK 8, US 6) needles and dark brown and black 2-ply (lace) yarn worked at the same time, cast on 4 sts. Work with both yarns together at the same time to create a random contrast of black speckles against the dark brown.

Row 1: inc 1, K2, inc 1 [6 sts].

Row 2: purl.

Row 3: inc 1, K to last st, inc 1 [8 sts].

Row 4: purl.

Row 5: inc 1, K to last st, inc 1 [10 sts].

Row 6–10: beginning with a purl row, work st st.

Row 11: K1, K2tog, K to last 3 sts, K2tog, K1 [8 sts].

Row 12: purl.

Row 13: K1, K2tog, K to last 3 sts, K2tog, K1 [6 sts]

Row 14: purl.

Row 15: K1, K2tog, K2tog, K1 [4 sts].

Row 15: purl.

Row 16: K2tog to end [2 sts].

Row 17: purl.

Cast off.

MAKING UP

Pull the thread tight at the top of the head and sew up the seam from the head to halfway down the belly. Stuff and sew up the remainder of the belly, then sew up the tail but do not stuff it. Sew the end seam of the tail so that it lies flat. Sew the wings into position on the body.

Cut out the bib from black felt, using the template, and sew it into position on chest, using black thread.

Cut out two beak triangles from black felt, using the template, and sew up two of the sides using black cotton thread. Squash the beak slightly to open it up and fatten it, then sew the open end to the head, using black thread. Next, sew the two beads onto the head for eyes, using black thread.

Follow the posable legs instruction on page 15 to create legs using 60cm (23½in) of copper wire, wrapping them with pink-brown thread.

Sparrow's wing placement and back markings

Sparrow templates

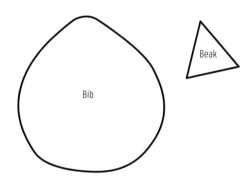

Bib

Beak

SEAGULL

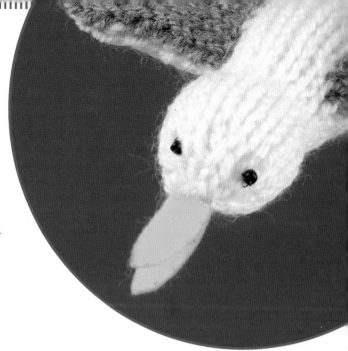

I live by the sea, and herring gulls are as much a part of coastal life as the waves and the beach. They are noisy, confident, and downright hilarious. Nothing is safe when the gull Mafia are in town – I have even seen them shoplifting from the local butchers.

Flying gulls, like these knitted ones, are graceful and peaceful to watch as they soar in the sky. It is when they land that the trouble starts!

Materials

- 10g (⅓oz) cream 8-ply (DK) yarn
- 5g (⅛oz) grey 8-ply (DK) yarn
- Small amount of black 8-ply (DK) yarn
- Yellow felt and matching cotton thread
- Two black seed beads
- Black cotton thread and sewing needle
- Chenille stems
- 122cm (48in) nylon thread
- Toy stuffing

Needles

- 4mm (UK 8, US 6) knitting needles

Tension

- 6 sts and 7 rows per 2.5cm (1in)

Size

- 14cm (5½in) from tip of beak to end of tail, 20cm (8in) from wingtip to wingtip

BODY AND HEAD

Worked in st st. Using 4mm (UK 8, US 6) needles and cream yarn, cast on 12 sts.

Row 1: knit.
Row 2: purl.
Row 3: *K2tog, K2, K2tog*, rep from * to * to end [8 sts].
Row 4: purl.
Row 5: K2tog to end [4 sts].
Row 6: purl.
Row 7: K1, inc in next 2 sts, K1 [6 sts].
Row 8: purl.
Row 9: *K1, inc 1, K1*, rep from * to * to end [8 sts].
Row 10: purl.
Row 11: *inc 1, K2, inc 1*, rep from * to * to end [12 sts].
Row 12: purl.
Row 13: *inc 1, K4, inc 1*, rep from * to * to end [16 sts].
Next rows: beginning with a purl row, work 19 rows in st st.
Row 33: K2tog to end [8 sts].
Row 34: purl.
Row 35: K2tog to end [4 sts].
Cut yarn, thread trailing end through remaining sts on needle.

WINGS

LEFT WING TOP (MAKE ONE)

Worked in st st. Using 4mm (UK 8, US 6) needles and grey yarn, cast on 10 sts.

Rows 1–6: beginning with a knit row, work st st.
Row 7: K1, inc 1, K to last 3 sts, K2tog, K1.
Row 8: purl.
Row 9: K1, inc 1, K to last 3 sts, K2tog, K1.
Row 10: purl.
Row 11: K1, K2tog, K to end [9 sts].
Row 12: purl.
Row 13: K1, K2tog, K to end [8 sts].
Row 14: purl.
Row 15: K1, K2tog, K to end [7 sts].
Row 16: purl.
Row 17: K1, K2tog, K to end [6 sts].
Row 18: purl.
Row 19: K1, K2tog, K to end [5 sts].
Row 20: purl.
Change to black yarn.
Row 21: K1, K2tog, K to end [4 sts].
Row 22: purl.
Row 23: K1, K2tog, K1 [3 sts].
Row 24: purl.
Row 25: K2tog, K1 [2 sts].
Cast off remaining 2 sts.

LEFT WING BOTTOM (MAKE ONE)

Worked in st st. Using 4mm (UK 8, US 6) needles and cream yarn, cast on 10 sts.

Rows 1–6: beginning with a knit row, work st st.
Row 7: K1, K2tog, K to last 2 sts, inc 1, K1.
Row 8: purl.
Row 9: K1, K2tog, K to last 2 sts, inc 1, K1.
Row 10: purl.
Row 11: K to last 3 sts, K2tog, K1 [9 sts].
Row 12: purl.
Row 13: K to last 3 sts, K2tog, K1 [8 sts].
Row 14: purl.
Row 15: K to last 3 sts, K2tog, K1 [7 sts].
Row 16: purl.
Row 17: K to last 3 sts, K2tog, K1 [6 sts].
Row 18: purl.
Row 19: K to last 3 sts, K2tog, K1 [5 sts].
Row 20: purl.
Change to black yarn.
Row 21: K to last 3 sts, K2tog, K1 [4 sts].
Row 22: purl.
Row 23: K1, K2tog, K1 [3 sts].
Row 24: purl.
Row 25: K1, K2tog [2 sts].
Cast off remaining 2 sts.

RIGHT WING TOP (MAKE ONE)

Work in the same way as the left wing bottom (see above), using grey yarn instead of cream. The black tip remains the same.

RIGHT WING BOTTOM (MAKE ONE)

Work in the same way as for the left wing top (see above) using cream yarn instead of grey. The black tip remains the same.

MAKING UP

Starting at the head, sew up the head and body seam, stuffing as you go. Do not stuff the tail or the narrow decrease section just before the tail. When you have sewn up the whole seam all the way to the end of the tail, position the body with the seam you have just sewn facing the bottom, then flatten the tail so it lies fanned out horizontally. Sew the seam across the end of the tail.

To create the neck shaping, run a thread through a row of stitches approximately 2.5cm (1in) from the tip of the head, and pull tight to create the shaping.

Each wing has a grey top and a cream underside. Take the left wing top and left wing bottom and oversew all round the edges using grey yarn, to seam the two pieces together, leaving the bottom, which joins to the body, open. Change to black yarn when you reach the tip. Repeat the process with the right wing top and right wing bottom. Bend a 15cm (6in) piece of chenille stem in half and insert it into the wing so the that two sharp ends stick approximately 2cm (¾in) out of the bottom of the wing.

Position the wing on the side of the body and poke the ends of the chenille stem into the body, adding stuffing to hold the wing in position. If the chenille stem pokes through to the other side of the body, trim it. Repeat with the other wing. When the wings are positioned to your liking, sew the wings into place on the body using grey yarn for the top of the wing and cream for the bottom.

Cut out two beak pieces from yellow felt, using the template. Sew together with yellow thread along the flat narrow end marked with a dotted line on the template – this is the end of the beak that will be attached to the head. Now sew the beak into position on the head, using yellow thread. Use black thread to sew the two black seed beads to the head as eyes.

To hang up, cut two 61cm (24in) lengths of invisible thread. Thread one through the back of the seagull's neck and one through the rear of the body. Use the threads to hang up your seagull.

Seagull beak template

RAVEN

The largest member of the crow family, ravens are often associated with death and disaster but also have a very playful side. They will roll down a snow-covered hill just for the fun of it!

Legend has it that if the ravens ever leave the Tower of London then disaster shall befall England. Maybe they should make a few of these knitted ravens and keep them at the Tower just to be on the safe side.

Materials

- ꝋ 60g (2oz) black 8-ply (DK) yarn
- ꝋ Four black chenille stems
- ꝋ 76cm (30in) 18 gauge wire
- ꝋ Two 5mm (¼in) black round beads
- ꝋ Small amount of black felt
- ꝋ Black cotton thread and sewing needle
- ꝋ Toy stuffing

Needles

- ꝋ 4mm (UK 8, US 6) knitting needles

Tension

- ꝋ 6 sts and 7 rows per 2.5cm (1in)

Size

- ꝋ 33cm (13in) from wingtip to wingtip, 21cm (8¼in) tall

Raven's eye and beak

Raven's feet

NOTES
The raven has wire support inside the tail, to help the bird stand up, and wire frames inside the wings, to keep them in the air.

BODY AND HEAD (MAKE ONE)
Worked in st st. Using 4mm (UK 8, US 6) needles and black yarn, cast on 28 sts.

Row 1: knit.

Row 2: purl.

Row 3: K5, K2tog, K2tog, K10, K2tog, K2tog, K5 [24 sts].

Row 4: purl.

Row 5: knit.

Row 6: purl.

Row 7: K4, K2tog, K2tog, K8, K2tog, K2tog, K4 [20 sts].

Row 8: purl.

Row 9: knit.

Row 10: purl.

Row 11: K3, K2tog, K2tog, K6, K2tog, K2tog, K3 [16 sts].

Row 12: purl.

Row 13: inc 1, K6, inc 2, K6, inc 1 [20 sts].

Row 14: purl.

Row 15: inc 1, K8, inc 2, K8, inc 1 [24 sts].

Row 16: purl.

Row 17: inc 1, K10, inc 2, K10, inc 1 [28 sts].

Row 18: purl.

Row 19: inc 1, K12, inc 2, K12, inc 1 [32 sts].

Row 20: purl.

Row 21: inc 1, K14, inc 2, K14, inc 1 [36 sts].

Rows 22–32: beginning with a purl row, work st st.

Row 33: *K2tog, K14, K2tog*, rep from * to * to end [32 sts].

Rows 34–40: beginning with a purl row, work st st.

Row 41: *K2tog, K12, K2tog*, rep from * to * to end [28 sts].

Rows 42–54: beginning with a purl row, work st st.

Row 55: K2tog to end [14 sts].

Row 56: purl.

Row 57: K2tog to end [7 sts].

Cut yarn, thread trailing end through remaining sts on needle.

WING PART 1 (MAKE TWO)

Worked in st st. Using 4mm (UK 8, US 6) needles and black yarn, cast on 14 sts.

Row 1: knit.
Row 2: purl.
Row 3: K1, inc 1, K10, inc 1, K1 [16 sts].
Row 4: purl.
Row 5: K1, inc 1, K12, inc 1, K1 [18 sts].
Row 6: purl.
Row 7: K1, inc 1, K14, inc 1, K1 [20 sts].
Row 8: purl.
Row 9: K1, inc 1, K16, inc 1, K1 [22 sts].
Row 10: purl.
Row 11: K1, inc 1, K18, inc 1, K1 [24 sts].
Row 12: purl.
Row 13: K1, inc 1, K20, inc 1, K1 [26 sts].
Row 14: purl.
Row 15: K1, K2tog, K18, K2tog, K2tog, K1 [23 sts].
Row 16: P1, P2tog, P2tog, P to end [21 sts].
Row 17: K1, K2tog, K13, K2tog, K2tog, K1 [18 sts].
Row 18: P1, P2tog, P2tog, P to end [16 sts].
Row 19: K1, K2tog, K8, K2tog, K2tog, K1 [13 sts].
Row 20: P1, P2tog, P2tog, P to end [11 sts].
Row 21: K1, K2tog, K3, K2tog, K2tog, K1 [8 sts].
Row 22: purl.
Row 23: K1, K2tog, K to end [7 sts].
Rows 24-26: beginning with a purl row, work st st.
Row 27: K1, K2tog, K to end [6 sts].
Rows 28-30: beginning with a purl row, work st st.
Row 31: K1, K2tog, K to end [5 sts].
Row 32: purl.
Row 33: K1, K2tog, K2 [4 sts].
Row 34: purl.
Row 35: K2tog to end [2 sts].
Cast off remaining sts.

WING PART 2 (MAKE TWO)

Worked in st st. Using 4mm (UK 8, US 6) needles and black yarn, cast on 14 sts.

Rows 1-14: work as for wing part 1.
Row 15: K1, K2tog, K2tog, K18, K2tog, K1 [23 sts].
Row 16: P18, P2tog, P2tog, P1 [21 sts].
Row 17: K1, K2tog, K2tog, K13, K2tog, K1 [18 sts].
Row 18: P13, P2tog, P2tog, P1 [16 sts].
Row 19: K1, K2tog, K2tog, K8, K2tog, K1 [13 sts].
Row 20: P8, P2tog, P2tog, P1 [11 sts].
Row 21: K1, K2tog, K2tog, K3, K2tog, K1 [8 sts].
Row 22: purl.

Row 23: K5, K2tog, K1 [7 sts].
Rows 24-26: beginning with a purl row, work st st.
Row 27: K4, K2tog, K1 [6 sts].
Rows 28-30: beginning with a purl row, work st st.
Row 31: K3, K2tog, K1 [5 sts].
Row 32: purl.
Row 33: K2, K2tog, K1 [4 sts].
Row 34: purl.
Row 35: K2tog to end [2 sts].
Cast off remaining sts.

LONG WING FEATHERS (MAKE FOUR)

Worked in st st. Using 4mm (UK 8, US 6) needles and black yarn, cast on 8 sts.

Rows 1-16: beginning with a knit row, work st st.
Row 17: K1, K2tog, K2, K2tog, K1 [6 sts].
Row 18: purl.
Row 19: K1, K2tog, K2tog, K1 [4 sts].
Row 20: purl.
Row 21: K2tog to end [2 sts].
Cast off remaining sts.

SHORT WING FEATHERS (MAKE FOUR)

Worked in st st. Using 4mm (UK 8, US 6) needles and black yarn, cast on 8 sts.

Rows 1-10: beginning with a knit row, work st st.
Row 11: K1, K2tog, K2, K2tog, K1 [6 sts].
Row 12: purl.
Row 13: K1, K2tog, K2tog, K1 [4 sts].
Row 14: purl.
Row 15: K2tog to end [2 sts].
Cast off remaining sts.

MAKING UP

Sew up the seam from the top of the head to the end of the tail, stuffing as you go. Do not sew up the seam at the end of the tail, where you cast on. Do not stuff the tail. Bend two 15cm (6in) chenille stems into the shape of the tail. Insert both into the tail, so you have a double thickness of chenille stem creating a framework inside the tail. Push the sharp chenille stem ends into the stuffing and then sew up the seam at the end of the tail. The chenille stems provide support to help the raven stand up.

Each of the wings uses one part 1 and one part 2, plus two long feathers and two short feathers. The top part of the left wing, and the bottom part of the right wing are both a part 2. Similarly, the top part of the right wing and the bottom part of the left wing are both made up of a part 1. Start by sewing up the side seam of each of the eight wing feathers.

To make the right wing, take one of the part 1 pieces and lay it flat on the table, wrong-side up. Take two black chenille stems and position them at the angle shown in the pictures, one up each side of the wing piece, pushing them through the back of some of the stitches near the edge of the wing piece to keep them in place. Trim the chenille stems so there are approximately 3.75cm (1½in) sticking out of the end of the wing that will join the body.

Take one of the part 2 pieces and position on top of part 1. Sew up the top seam from A to B, and the bottom seam from C to D, sandwiching the chenille stems between the two wing pieces. Leave the rest of the wing seam open.

Insert wing feathers into the unsewn seam, between B and D: the two longer feathers at the top and the shorter ones at the bottom. When you are happy with the positioning, pin the feathers into place and sew up the seam from B to D to secure the feathers in place.

To make the left wing, take the remaining part 2 piece and repeat the construction process for the right wing (see above), inserting chenille sticks and sewing wing part 1 onto the top.

Before sewing the wings into position on the body, push the sharp ends of the chenille stems that are sticking out of the base of the wings into the body, making sure that they are pushed deep within the body stuffing. Sew the wings into position on the body.

Follow the posable legs instruction on page 15 to create legs using a 76cm (30in) piece of stiff craft wire, wrapped in black 8-ply (DK) yarn. Bend the wire so that each toe is approximately 2.5cm (1in) long, and each leg is 2.5cm (1in) tall.

Cut out two beak pieces from black felt, using the templates. Sew the two pieces together, using black cotton, leaving the end that will be attached to the head open. Gently stuff with polyester stuffing and sew to the head using black cotton. To finish, sew two black beads onto the head, for eyes, using black cotton.

Detail of the raven's wing, showing the reference for chenille stem placement and sewing up

Detail of the point where the wings join the body

Raven beak templates

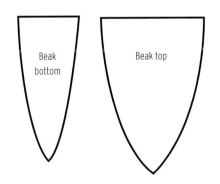

Beak
bottom

Beak top

TUFTED DUCK

I often spot these smart little black and white diving ducks at my local Wetlands Trust. They suddenly dive under the water and – just when you think they're not coming back up again – up they pop, quite a distance away.

Materials

- 10g (⅓oz) black 8-ply (DK) yarn
- Small amounts of cream 8-ply (DK) yarn
- Two 4mm (³⁄₁₆in) yellow glass seed beads and matching cotton thread
- Grey felt and matching cotton thread
- Sewing needle
- 3mm (UK 11, US C/D) crochet hook
- Toy stuffing

Needles

- 4mm (UK 8, US 6) knitting needles

Tension

- 6 sts and 7 rows per 2.5cm (1in)

Size

- 11cm (4¼in) wide, 9cm (3½in) tall

NOTES

The colours in parentheses indicate the yarn you should use for the stitches that follow.

The pattern contains notes on working with two balls of yarn for certain sections. Doing so makes your working easier because you do not have to carry the yarn across the back of the section.

BODY (MAKE ONE)

Worked in st st. Using 4mm (UK 8, US 6) needles and black yarn, cast on 8 sts.

Row 1: *inc 1, K2, inc 1*, rep from * to * to end [12 sts].

Row 2: purl.

Row 3: *inc 1, K4, inc 1*, rep from * to * to end [16 sts].

Row 4: purl.

Row 5: *inc 1, K6, inc 1*, rep from * to * to end [20 sts].

Row 6: purl.

Row 7: *inc 1, K8, inc 1*, rep from * to * to end [24 sts].

Row 8: purl.

From row 9 onwards, work with two balls of cream yarn.

Row 9: (cream) K5, (black) inc 2, K10, inc 2, (cream) K5 [28 sts].

Row 10: purl, keeping colour sequence.

Row 11: (cream) K6, (black) inc 2, K12, inc 2, (cream) K6 [32 sts].

Rows 12–14: beginning with a purl row, work st st, keeping the colour sequence throughout.

Row 15: (cream) K7, (black) inc 2, K14, inc 2, (cream) K7 [36 sts].

Rows 16–20: beginning with a purl row, work st st, keeping the colour sequence throughout.

Work all in black from this point to the end.

Row 21: K7, K2tog, K2tog, K14, K2tog, K2tog, K7 [32 sts].

Row 22: purl.

Row 23: K6, K2tog, K2tog, K12, K2tog, K2tog, K6 [28 sts].

Row 24: purl.

Row 25: K5, K2tog, K2tog, K10, K2tog, K2tog, K5 [24 sts].

Row 26: purl.

Row 27: K4, K2tog, K2tog, K8, K2tog, K2tog, K4 [20 sts].

Row 28: purl.

Row 29: K2tog to end [10 sts].

Cut yarn, thread trailing end through remaining sts on needle.

HEAD (MAKE ONE)

Worked in st st. Using 4mm (UK 8, US 6) needles and black yarn, cast on 20 sts.

Rows 1–10: beginning with a knit row, work st st.

Row 11: K2tog to end [10 sts].

Row 12: purl.

Cut yarn, thread trailing end through remaining sts on needle.

RIGHT WING (MAKE ONE)

Worked in st st. Using 4mm (UK 8, US 6) needles and black yarn, cast on 4 sts.

Row 1: K1, inc 2, K1 [6 sts].

Row 2: purl.

Row 3: (black) K1, inc 1, (cream) K2, inc 1, K1 [8 sts].

Row 4: purl, keeping colour sequence.

Row 5: (black) K1, inc 1, K1, (cream) K3, inc 1, K1 [10 sts].

Row 6: purl, keeping colour sequence.

Row 7: (black) K1, inc 1, K3, (cream) K3, inc 1, K1 [12 sts].

Row 8: purl, keeping colour sequence.

Row 9: (black) K1, inc 1, K5, (cream) K3, inc 1, K1 [14 sts].

Rows 10–12: beginning with a purl row, work st st, keeping the colour sequence throughout.

Row 13: (black) K1, K2tog, K4, (cream) K4, K2tog, K1 [12 sts].

Row 14: purl, keeping colour sequence.

Row 15: (black) K1, K2tog, K2, (cream) K4, K2tog, K1 [10 sts].

Row 16: purl, keeping colour sequence.

Row 17: (black) K1, K2tog, K2, (cream) K2, K2tog, K1 [8 sts].

Row 18: purl, keeping colour sequence.

Work all in black from this point to the end of the wing.

Row 19: K1, K2tog, K2, K2tog, K1 [6 sts].

Row 20: purl.

Row 21: K1, K2tog, K2tog, K1 [4 sts].

Row 22: purl.

Row 23: K2tog to end [2 sts].

Cast off remaining sts.

LEFT WING (MAKE ONE)

Worked in st st. Using 4mm (UK 8, US 6) needles and black yarn, cast on 4 sts.

Row 1: K1, inc 2, K1 [6 sts].

Row 2: purl.

Row 3: (cream) K1, inc 1, K2, (black) inc 1, K1 [8 sts].

Row 4: purl, keeping colour sequence.

Row 5: (cream) K1, inc 1, K3, (black) K1, inc 1, K1 [10 sts].

Row 6: purl, keeping colour sequence.

Row 7: (cream) K1, inc 1, K3, (black) K3, inc 1, K1 [12 sts].

Row 8: purl, keeping colour sequence.

Row 9: (cream), K1, inc 1, K3, (black) K5, inc 1, K1 [14 sts].

Rows 10–12: beginning with a purl row, work st st, keeping the colour sequence throughout.

Row 13: (cream) K1, K2tog, K4, (black) K4, K2tog, K1 [12 sts].

Row 14: purl, keeping colour sequence.

Row 15: (cream) K1, K2tog, K4, (black) K2, K2tog, K1 [10 sts].

Row 16: purl, keeping colour sequence.

Row 17: (cream) K1, K2tog, K2, (black) K2, K2tog, K1 [8 sts].

Row 18: purl, keeping colour sequence.

Work all in black from this point to end of wing.

Row 19: K1, K2tog, K2, K2tog, K1 [6 sts].

Row 20: purl.

Row 21: K1, K2tog, K2tog, K1 [4 sts].

Row 22: purl.

Row 23: K2tog to end [2 sts].

Cast off remaining sts.

MAKING UP

Sew up the body seam, leaving a space to stuff. The end where you ran a thread through the remaining stitches on the needle is the head end of the body. Stuff the body, then sew up the remainder of the seam.

Sew up the head side seam, leaving the bottom open. Stuff the head and then run a thread through the last row of stitches and pull tight to draw the bottom closed and create a nice rounded head shape. Sew the head onto the body using the pictures for positioning reference.

Sew the wings onto the body, leaving the wing tips loose. The white wing flashes should be at the bottom of the wing.

Cut out two grey felt beak shapes using the templates, overstitch together using grey cotton thread, leaving the end that will attach to the head open. Stuff the beak with a little polyester stuffing and sew to the head. Sew two yellow beads on to the head for eyes.

To create the tuft, cut two 12.75cm (5in) strands of black 8-ply (DK) yarn. Fold in half, hook them with the crochet hook and pull through the top of the head. Take the four ends of the two pieces of yarn and push them through the loop made by folding the two pieces in half. Pull tight to secure. Trim the thread until the yarn forms tufts approximately 2.5cm (1in) in length to finish.

Tufted duck's head

Tufted duck bill templates

Top of bill

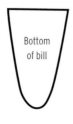

Bottom of bill

EGGS AND NESTS

If your knitted birds are looking for somewhere to rest, why not knit them a nest or two? They may even lay some knitted eggs in them. The smaller nest will be the right size for blackbirds, robins, blue tits and sparrows, while the larger nest is perfect for a magpie. You can fill it with sparkly treasures or even let the magpie look after your house keys and loose change.

Materials

Magpie egg:
- Small amount of slate blue 8-ply (DK) yarn
- Small amount of black 2-ply (lace) yarn
- Toy stuffing

Blackbird egg:
- Small amount of light blue 2-ply (lace) yarn
- Small amount of light brown embroidery thread
- Toy stuffing

Needles

Magpie egg:
- 4mm (UK 8, US 6) knitting needles

Blackbird egg:
- 3mm (UK 11, US 2/3) knitting needles

Tension

Magpie egg:
- 5 sts and 8 rows per 2.5cm (1in)

Blackbird egg:
- 8 sts and 10 rows per 2.5cm (1in)

Size

Magpie egg:
- 6.5cm (2½in) long

Blackbird egg:
- 3.75cm (1½in) long

EGGS

> ### NOTES
> Both the magpie and blackbird eggs are worked with the same pattern.

EGG

Worked in st st. Using the needles and yarn specified in the list of materials, cast on 7 sts. If you are knitting the magpie egg, work both yarns together at the same time – the black 2-ply (lace) yarn creates a speckled effect.

Row 1: inc in every stitch to end [14 sts].
Row 2: purl.
Row 3: *K1, inc 1*, rep from * to * to end [21 sts].
Rows 4–14: beginning with a purl row, work st st.
Row 15: *K1, K2tog*, rep from * to * to end [14 sts].
Row 16: purl.
Row 17: K2tog to end [7 sts].
Row 18: purl.
Run yarn through remaining sts on needle.

MAKING UP

For both magpie and blackbird eggs, the cast-on edge creates the flat end of the egg. Fold the egg in half, sew the cast-on edge together using overstitch, then sew up the rest of the egg seam using mattress stitch, stuffing as you go.

To finish the blackbird egg, embroider a random scattering of speckles, using two strands of embroidery thread. If you want to copy mother nature, make sure that there are more speckles at the rounded end of the egg!

The relative sizes of the eggs

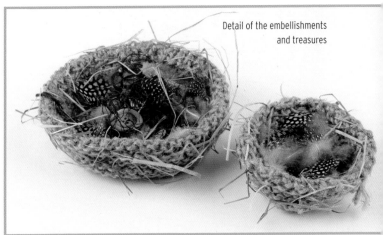
Detail of the embellishments
and treasures

Blackbird eggs
and nest

Magpie eggs
and nest

Materials

- ↯ 70g (2½oz) garden twine (sufficient to make both nests)
- ↯ Oddments of straw and dried grass
- ↯ Sharp darning needle
- ↯ Feathers
- ↯ For the magpie's nest: vintage silver coins, keys, treasures and textured yarn

Needles

- ↯ 5.5mm (UK 5, US 9) knitting needles

Tension

Magpie nest:
- ↯ 3 sts and 3 rows per 2.5cm (1in)

Blackbird nest:
- ↯ 3 sts and 3 rows per 2.5cm (1in)

Size

Magpie nest:
- ↯ 17.75cm (7in) diameter

Blackbird nest:
- ↯ 11.25cm (4½in) diameter

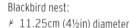

NESTS

NOTES

Do not use your best bamboo knitting needles for this project. Jute twine is rough and tough, so use an old pair of metal knitting needles and keep your stitches loose to make it easier to knit with.

Because you are knitting a loose shape, the tension is not as important for the nests as the other projects. You can easily stretch the nest into shape once you are finished.

Please, please do not use real wild birds' eggs to fill your nest! If you do not want to use knitted eggs, quail's eggs – available from supermarkets – look great nestled in the nest, or you might use them to hold chocolate eggs instead.

BLACKBIRD'S NEST

Worked in garter st. Using 5.5mm (UK 5, US 9) needles and jute twine, cast on 30 sts.

Initial rows: Work in garter st until work measures 6.5cm (2½in) from cast-on edge.

Next row: *K1, K2tog*,rep from * to * to end [20 sts].

Next row: knit.

Next row: K1, *K1, K2tog*, rep from * to * to last st, K1 [14 sts].

Next row: knit.

> **Next row:** K2tog to end [7 sts].
>
> Run yarn through remaining sts.

MAGPIE'S NEST

Worked in garter st. Using 5.5mm (UK 5, US 9) needles and jute twine, cast on 50 sts.

Initial rows: work in garter st until work measures 10cm (4in) from cast-on edge.

Next row: K1, *K1, K2tog*, rep from * to * to last st, K1 [34 sts].

Next row: knit.

Next row: K1, *K1, K2tog*, rep from * to * to end [23 sts].

Next row: knit.

Next row: K1, *K1, K2tog*, rep from * to * to last st, K1 [16 sts].

Next row: knit.

Next row: K2tog to end [8 sts].

Run yarn through remaining sts.

MAKING UP

Sew up the seam, and then use your fingers to pull the nest into shape. You can shape your nest to have a flat bottom if you want it to sit on a flat surface, or a more rounded bottom if it is going to sit in a tree.

Using a sharp darning needle, weave pieces of dried grass and straw through the loops of your knitting. Line your nest with a few soft feathers (I used guinea fowl feathers) and place your eggs in your nest.

The magpie's nest is made up in the same way, but you can line the nest with a few strands of textured yarn as well as the feathers. Add treasures!

Acknowledgements

Thanks to Sarah Best, Creative Waves Community Art,
Emyr Evans and the Dyfi Osprey Project, Daniela Gargiulo,
Russell Jeanes, Claudia Marioglou, Heidi Mitchell,
Robert Newman, Kaye Richardson, Ally Tarwater,
Patricia Warren and the WWT Arundel Wetland Centre,
and all the Worthing Meet and Makers.